ANTI-RACIST PSYCHOTHERAPY

CONFRONTING SYSTEMIC RACISM AND HEALING RACIAL TRAUMA

DAVID ARCHER

EACH ONE
TEACH ONE
PUBLICATIONS

Anti-Racist Psychotherapy: Confronting Systemic Racism and Healing Racial Trauma

David Archer

Note: All individuals presented in story segments are based on composites. Fictional descriptions have been used in order to maintain confidentiality. The information provided in this book should not be treated as a substitute for professional medical or clinical advice; always consult a medical or clinical practitioner. Any use of this book is at the reader's discretion or risk. Neither the author nor the publisher can be held responsible for any loss, claim, or damage arising out of the use, or misuse, of the suggestions made, the failure to take medical or clinical advice, or for any material on third-party websites or references.

First Printing: February 2021

ISBN: 978-1-7774504-3-4

Portions of this book were originally published as Archer, D. (2020). Racial Trauma, Neurons, and EMDR: The Path Towards an Anti-Racist Psychotherapy. *Go With That Magazine.*

David Archer
PO BOX 99900 QS 788 797
RPO WEST HILL
MONTRÉAL QC H4B 0A3
david@archertherapy.com
www.antiracistpsychotherapy.com

David Archer is available to speak at your business or conference event on a variety of topics. Send an email to david@archertherapy.com **for booking information.**

WHY READ THIS BOOK

This book may be the first to discuss anti-racism from a scientific and family-systems based approach. It also explores the neurobiological implications of racial trauma.

The purpose of anti-racist psychotherapy is to explain the societal function of anti-Black racism and to equip the reader with strategies to reprocess the mental health consequences of it.

With this book, the reader will acquire a knowledgebase for becoming more authentic, more aware, and more committed to social change.

Raising our racial consciousness allows people of all cultural backgrounds to be more fully equipped to stop the trauma of racism.

I have put my heart into writing this, and I pass on all that I know to you. Let us have courage, be open-minded, and move toward a better future.

MINDFULNESS INFORMED, INTERSECTIONAL, SYSTEMS-BASED PSYCHOTHERAPIST

D avid Archer is an anti-racist psychotherapist, EMDRIA certified EMDR practitioner, a certified Brainspotting therapist, clinical social worker, couple and family therapist, and mindfulness meditator from Montreal, Canada (Tiohtià:ke). He is an expert clinician who works in private practice with diverse clinical populations. Archer provides both individual and group consultation to other therapists in training. He specializes in efficient psychotherapeutic interventions that are designed to maintain long-lasting changes.

David Archer co-presented the ground-breaking plenary discussion *Elephant In The Room: Racism and Psychotherapy*, led anti-racist workshops at both EMDRIA and ISSTD world conferences, as well as participated in numerous panel discussions and peer supervisions in local community circles. He has years of experience working with a range of clients who suffer from racial trauma, child abuse, anxiety, depressive disorders, relational conflict, addictions, and eating disorders. In addition to extensive work with immigrants and racial minorities, he spent several years as a counselor in the Native American community of Kahnawake, where he cultivated a deeper understanding of the culture, community, and the spirit of resilience.

David Archer provides expert consultation to professionals regarding anti-Black racism, trauma resolution, and minority stress. When not writing about these topics, he enjoys listening to deep house music and roots and culture reggae while cruising on the highway. He enjoys eating spicy food like it's his day job, and in his spare time, he plays very difficult indie/Japanese anime video games. He believes that people learn best while having fun—even when approaching challenging topics.

When you have finished reading this book, you will develop a deeper understanding of race relations. It is hoped that this experience will be as enriching as it will be thought-provoking.

To invite David Archer as a speaker at your next event or conference, email him at David@archertherapy.com **or visit** www.antiracistpsychotherapy.com.

ADVANCE PRAISE FOR *ANTI-RACIST PSYCHOTHERAPY*

"David Archer shares great insights on race relations, mental health, and how to heal from trauma. Buy this now!"

Resmaa Menakem, MSW, LICSW, SEP
Author of My Grandmother's Hands: Racialized Trauma and the
Pathway to Mending Our Hearts and Bodies

"This book presents a valuable and important clinical resource, not only for working with visible minorities but all client groups. It is a powerful and challenging text offering a necessary invitation to examine your own therapeutic approach and personal ideologies. As such, it is an essential read for all helping professionals."

Tom Caplan, MSW, MFT
Adjunct Professor at McGill University's School of Social Work
Consultant to the McGill Domestic Violence Clinic
Founder of the Montreal Anger Management Centre

"David Archer's book skillfully addresses one of the most urgent issues of our age – racism. We are on the cusp of a paradigm change as racism and other forms of discrimination take center stage as fundamental mental health considerations. This book is a must-read for therapists everywhere."

Michael Salter, PhD
Scientia Associate Professor

"In his book, David Archer provides an accessible, yet extensively researched pathway for those interested in integrating anti-racist tenets with psychotherapy. As a social work professor, I have been waiting for a book like this! Drawing from his educational and practice experiences, Archer demonstrates the practical relevance and urgency to integrate critical race theory into psychotherapeutic approaches, particularly when working with Black, Indigenous, and other People of Color (BIPOC) individuals. By contextualizing trauma, and in particular racial trauma stemming from anti-Black racism, within the mental health impacts of systemic and intersectional forms of racism, Archer presents a cogent analytical and applied framework for anti-racist psychotherapy. This book is not only useful for psychotherapists but also general community members who wish to gain insight into how to engage in an anti-racist approach to psychotherapy."

Edward Lee, PhD
Associate Professor School of Social Work, Université de Montréal

"In this provocative book, David Archer introduces the reader to essential elements of Critical Race Theory, Mindfulness meditation, and EMDR therapy. His goal is to delineate the foundation for an Anti-Racist approach to psychotherapy. In this endeavor, he has taken essential first steps. The book is not a detailed psychotherapy guide, but rather is a personal and philosophical investigation that challenges clinicians to step outside the limits of their collective cultural trauma and explore new ground with him."

Andrew M. Leeds, Ph.D.
Director of Training Sonoma Psychotherapy Training Institute
Author of *A Guide to the Standard EMDR Therapy Protocols for Clinicians, Supervisors, and Consultants, 2nd Edition*

"I met David Archer in 2020, a year like no other in my experience. David is also a man like no other in many ways. He is an experienced EMDR therapist, an anti-racist psychotherapist from Montreal, Canada, and I have been impressed with him since that first virtual meeting. David speaks in a way that is clear and understandable, knowledgeable, and passionate. In his new book, he has hit the nail on the head with his ideas on anti-racist psychotherapy, presenting without needless jargon, the tools we need to work effectively in the real world we live in today. Therapists can benefit from his analysis of the literature and his experience as an EMDR therapist himself. Trauma therapists will want to add this book to their resource library now!"

Carol Miles, LCSW
EMDRIA Past President, EMDR Certified Therapist, EMDRIA
Approved Consultant, and EMDR Therapy Trainer

"David Archer displays a profound understanding of the intersection between relations, mental health, and trauma recovery. This book is a must-read for everyone dedicated to treating underserved populations."

Heather Hall, MD
Board Certified Psychiatrist Specializing in Psychotherapy and
Medication Management

"A refreshing and insightful exploration of what may very well be the most important issue of our times. David Archer is a gifted psychotherapist, and his book Anti-Racist Psychotherapy offers new insights into how systemic racism and trauma can be addressed in therapy and lead to genuine healing."

Soham Rej MD, MSc, Psychiatrist
Jewish General Hospital
McGill University

"David Archer's book is a welcomed and much-needed guide to an intentionally anti-racist approach to psychotherapy. He skillfully integrates his lived experience as a Black man and psychotherapist with foundational concepts in critical race theory and anti-racism. From this platform, he reviews current psychotherapy approaches to recommend how they can be better informed, modified, or discarded. His analysis includes fresh and original thoughts and an unmistakably human voice with a vision of what is possible."

Mark Nickerson, LICSW
Cultural Competence and Healing Culturally Based Trauma with
EMDR Therapy: Insights, Strategies and Protocols (Springer, 2016)

"David Archer interrupts our complacency with a brilliant yet humble challenge, not only to psychotherapists but to any professionals willing to explore assumptions about being black in our predominantly white society. He explores the systemic roots of suffering and racist thinking. This well-researched book not only weaves mindfulness and family systems with adverse childhood experiences, but it also covers other traumas, with helpful methods of treating our unconscious biases leading us to a deeper understanding of both racism and ourselves."

C. Paul Peel, R. Psych., RMFT, BCETS
Registered Psychologist, EMDRIA Approved Consultant
Member, IASP, Participant in WHO Field Studies
Founding Member of EMDRIA

"For anyone who wants to understand Critical Race Theory and how it applies to today's events, this book by David Archer is a good place to start."

Dr. Myrna Lashley
Assistant professor in McGill University's department of psychiatry
Researcher at Lady Davis Institute for Medical Research of the
Jewish General Hospital

"David Archer, relying on his own experiences and the theorizing and research of many other mental health professionals, provides a valuable and important contribution to the field of racial justice in general and, more specifically, the need for therapists to take this issue to heart for both their clients and for themselves. He provides many perspectives and specific approaches on how to do this. The struggle with racism has been marked by a pattern of 'three steps forward, two steps back' for the last century. The historical problem has been the sometimes smug assumption that the problem is with other people; the problem, to one degree or another, is with all of us, and that includes mental health professionals. As David so clearly shows, our profession grants us no immunity from the problem and, in fact, requires a special responsibility on our part. This book should be mandatory reading for all who wish to be psychotherapists and a clear tool for those who want to be better at their work and their lives."

Steven M. Silver, Ph.D.
Certified Clinician, Approved Consultant, EMDR International

Association Facilitator and Senior Trainer, EMDR Institute First Programs Chairperson, EMDR Humanitarian Assistance Programs Coauthor, *Light in the heart of darkness: EMDR and the treatment of war and terrorism survivors*

"Given the recent global protests and push-backs surrounding systemic racism, this book is timely. Pertinent for professionals and the lay public, it explains how racism works, how it affects racialized groups, and how to heal from systemic discrimination. The author, David Archer, makes no apologies for his very lucid insights regarding the need for anti-racist psychotherapy as the only valid approach for healing trauma anchored in repetitive exposure to racism.

The book illustrates what marginalized individuals and groups recognize, that they do not fit into most mental health treatment models offered by mainstream institutions, which are themselves sites of systemic oppressive practices. The chapter on anti-racist EMDR approach is insightful. As a clinician with more than 20 years of practice working with complex trauma, there are instances where talk therapy is not enough. Those occasions are opportunities to utilize other therapeutic models such as EMDR, hypnosis, or other mindfulness approaches.

This enormous undertaking encourages clinicians, educators to actively reject oppressive mental health therapeutic practices and implore them to discover alternative treatment approaches that are responsive to race, culture, and the context of their students, clients, and patients. The process of decolonization is incomplete and continues to be a formidable task for both colonizer and colonized. Strategies need to be developed with regard to exploring and accepting other narratives. Only then as Archer proposes will clinicians working with traumatized blacks be in a position to help them get from a place of enduring to one of healing."

Shirlette Wint, MSW
Clinical Social Worker
Licensed Psychotherapist

TABLE OF CONTENTS

PREFACE:

AN INTRODUCTION TO ANTI-RACISM

We must solve the problem of anti-Black racism.

First Trauma

My first traumatic encounter occurred at the age of five. I was cycling on my bright red tricycle. Even though I had little knowledge of what race meant at that moment, I would soon come to realize just how significant our differences can be.

During that autumn evening, the wind shifted against the trees as the sun gently receded and darkness loomed. My red tricycle twisted and turned in circles in front of my home over and over again to my excitement as my parents took turns to supervise me. As the light of the day began to dim, I noticed a group of White teenagers. Their sneers, the foul language, their shaved heads, all of it was foreign to me.

As one of my parents went inside to switch turns supervising, I remained the only member of my family outside. This group of fierce-looking teenagers noticed that. My circles grew wider, and the perimeter of my cycling expanded. All of a sudden, the group took issue with this liberty. One of the biggest and meanest teenagers clenched his fist, moved toward me, and spat in my face.

While I did not understand what had happened, I knew that that was an act of aggression. I cried and wept and ran inside.

"Daddy," I cried as he leaped up instinctually, enraged at this violation of my safety on his watch. He did what any protective parent would do, he grabbed a baseball bat and sought to confront this group of cowards. The neighbors called the police on my father. Although no charges were laid, I learned at that time that the world could be unsafe. However, those in positions of authority have a responsibility to protect the public. My father did what he could to protect me, and the police maintained the peace. All was well and as it should be in Quebec, Canada.

The Rationale

Now bringing it back to the present, there is an even greater bully confronting our young ones. As I write this, we live in a world that has been confronted by the dual pandemic: the virus of COVID-19 and the sickness of systemic racism. Both of these tend to have severe complications as their viral load becomes more virulent. But while we may be able to prevent a virus with the prick of a needle, the global pandemic of systemic racism is much more difficult to eradicate.

This renewed interest in talking about systemic racism has been spurred on by the public lynching of many notable brothers and sisters. George Floyd's death at the knee of a police officer was especially symbolic in that it was recorded on video that would eventually go viral. The public murder was replayed millions of times around the world. We say Black Lives Matter because Black life is not equal to White life in a society that privileges being White over being Black; neutrality is a fallacy.

We must solve the problem of anti-Black racism. I emphasize racism toward Black people because all other people are caught up in this false dichotomy of good and evil, of Whiteness and Blackness, of light and dark.

Whiteness is held to be justice and the ideal, while my skin color represents deviance and malevolence. This sickness needs to stop, and we are all implicated. The only way to achieve this is by removing the cultural taboos about discussing racial trauma, training better therapists/change-workers, and having the courage to act despite our fear.

Much has been discussed about the impact of systemic racism in the past few months. Still, there are not as many people talking about the psychological consequences of our repeated exposure to racial trauma. Trauma is rarely discussed when countries decide to go to war or when refugees come to our borders. We rarely address the trauma caused by social or political events. We are training people to dissociate from trauma and see healing from it as unlikely or, worse, impossible.

Racism is endemic in North America, and it can influence not only the police officers but all professionals, including teachers, psychologists, and employers. Any occupation which has the capacity to determine who "passes" and who "fails" is susceptible to the biases of racism. The guy who spat on me could very well be in a management position to this day or even one day be the president of the United States. He could even be someone's therapist. You never know where these bigoted people end up. However, we need to get over this misconception that only the police officers are guilty of racism while you and I are not susceptible to abuse of power.

I write this knowing that many people will disagree with me, but there is so much at stake, and if this understanding can save even one life, I will have accomplished my task.

Thus, I would like to sound a note of fair warning in advance. Many of the terms I use in this book may cause various feelings from rage or anger to disgust. Not all White people are racist, but all non-Black people benefit from anti-Black racism. This is because the trauma of White supremacy harms Black people and ensnares even those who happen to be White. Consequently, we must all seek to eliminate it together and forever. Therefore, let us be brave and undertake this journey together.

The Basic Premise

"In a racist society it is not enough to be non-racist, we must be anti-racist." — Angela Davis

Racism was once created, and, as such, it can also be destroyed. The true nature of racism is systemic and trauma-based. We have all the theories we need to get to the root of this. What I have written is a compilation of my own research and clinical practice. These are perspectives, tools, and approaches from various sources that have made differences in the lives of thousands. I endeavor to share them with the world to set a foundation of individuals who can build on it and advance it. Anti-racist psychotherapy is not just mine; it also belongs to the people who seek to heal the trauma of racism.

Nevertheless, the key is that we cannot just do another course on cultural competency or another course on "diversity and inclusion" or whatever any of that means. Our cultural competency has failed us in that we claim to know others without truly knowing ourselves. We need an updated cultural foundation that is both anti-racist and is trauma-informed.

This book is written for the change workers, those of you who have been affected by racism and want to make a difference. You can be of any race and be an anti-racist. White supremacy is fatal to all of us, and even non-White people can be White Supremacists.

As Dr. Kendi writes, racism is not only behavioral, but it also affects and is affected by our socio-political context. We either support policies that are anti-racist or policies that are racist; there is no ability for us to be non-racist in a society based on race.[1] And as Mr. Menakem explains, suffering is stored deep in our nervous systems. In addition to Black people being affected, White people also suffer from the effects of "White body supremacy."[2] And Dr. Degruy explains that the multi-generational impact of slavery still has

---

[1]Kendi, I. X. (2019). *How to be an Antiracist*. One World.
[2]Menakem, R. (2017). *My Grandmother's Hands: Racialized trauma and the Pathway to Mending our Hearts and Bodies*. Central Recovery Press.

ripple effects to this day, contributing to the deep levels of internalized oppression and the detrimental impacts of surviving such horrors.[3]

I write in a spirit of pulling together the ideas of those giants who have preceded me. We all seek the same goal of making the world stronger together.

Anti-racist Psychotherapy is exactly as its name suggests; it is an approach that is meant to eliminate the suffering caused by this socially constructed sickness by treating the mind, body, and spirit of those impacted by it.

Because racism is systemically impacting individuals and communities simultaneously, anti-racism must also be as self-reflective as it is goal-directed. No person has not suffered under the sickness of racism either directly or indirectly. By reading this work, I will do my best to ensure that you have the appropriate vocabulary and understanding to navigate the chasms of this scourge. You will also be able to view mental health through a trauma-informed and anti-racist perspective. I will also provide you with anti-racist perspectives on some psychotherapeutic approaches and interventions designed to eliminate the trauma caused by White supremacy and Black suffering.

I have put my heart into referring to the research available, writing with my fellow scientist-practitioners in mind. However, even those who are not therapists can still benefit from understanding the science behind how we can recover from pathogenic memories and the mechanisms behind brain-based interventions, which can help us to resolve the problem of racial trauma.

Simply put, in learning about this approach, I hope to help even you, the reader, to understand that we can heal ourselves and help others heal from these socially constructed means of suffering.

Thank you for taking the time to read this.
Let's give it our best shot.

---

[3]DeGruy, J. (2005). *Post Traumatic Slave Syndrome*. Portland: Joy De Gruy Publications Inc.

PART ONE:

THE FOUNDATIONAL PRINCIPLES OF ANTI-RACIST PSYCHOTHERAPY

CHAPTER 1:

TOWARD SOLVING THE PROBLEM OF ANTI-BLACK RACISM

Skin Like Dirt

"Oww!" I said as I pulled back my arm. The grade-school children laughed amongst themselves. They were practicing what they called "Indian sunburns," a practice where one child would take another kid's arm and attempt to pull or twist the skin in two different directions. The children took turns grabbing one another's forearms, looking at the red marks that would appear after releasing their grips. They all laughed at the pain inflicted.

No such marks appeared on mine. I did not understand why it was called an "Indian" sunburn or why this was a form of entertainment. I kept my distance. One of the other kids noticed I did not have a red mark on my skin and jeered; the others laughed.

"It's still black," a boy said.

"Maybe it's because his skin is like dirt; we have to wash it off first," another kid remarked. They laughed, and I backed away from them.

> I refused to play their games. I was not like them. I could never be like them.
>
> I was given a Blackness that could never come off.

Despite the innocence of children, from an early age, we are taught to notice differences between others. But what is the function and impact of our racial differences? I will attempt to discuss race, its social functions, and the effect it plays on all people caught up in the binary concept of "Black" and "White."

Is Race Real?

To explain race, I like to use a cultural icon, Stevie Wonder.[4] He is a world-renowned artist who opposes the view of seeing blindness or being "racialized" as a disadvantage. People who are disabled are rarely discussed or given a voice in the media and so are often considered a marginalized group. But Stevie Wonder is unique in that he is a high-profile artistic genius who happens to be both "blind" and "Black." Oftentimes too, we live in a world where the title of Black is seen as insignificant or undesirable compared to the title of White. However, his case is important in that he is a person who has high self-esteem despite these labels given to him. Does the concept of Black exist to a person who cannot see the label? Is Black real? While the challenges of blindness are, in some cases, biological, the categorizations of race are not substantiated by science and are not uniformly supported by geneticists.

Rutherford[5] explains that this idea of "White" racial dominance is based on pseudoscience and that any concept of racial "purity" is nonsense. It is understood that all human beings share common ancestors from the African continent. He explains that race as taxonomy is not well

---

[4]Lester, P. (2012, August 30). Stevie Wonder: 'I never thought of being blind and black as a disadvantage'. *The Guardian.*
https://www.theguardian.com/music/2012/aug/30/stevie-wonder-blind-black-disadvantage

[5]Rutherford, A. (2020). *How to Argue with a Racist: History, Science, Race and Reality.* Hachette UK.

supported by our current understandings of biology or evolution. Having rhythm or excelling in sports has nothing to do with being Black, while Asian students do not excel in science because of their country's flag.

These stereotypes are racist for a reason because they discount hard work, determination, and resilience. But whether or not it is real, there are real consequences to race. Here we must consider differential outcomes depending on race.

Differential Outcomes for Racial Minorities

On multiple levels, racial minorities encounter societal problems differently from members of the majority racial group. For example, in consideration of violence against women, much research describes the extent to which gendered violence is widespread in the world across cultures, ethnic groups, and different races.[6] However, even in domestic violence cases, some writers suggest that the media often associates domestic violence in higher proportions to racial minorities.[7] Also, it is not only the media's conceptions; researchers have often indicated that there are higher proportions of Black women in comparison to Whites who are victims of gendered violence.[8] In Canada, much research has pointed toward an overrepresentation of incidences of violence toward women of color and specifically toward Aboriginal women.[9]

Additionally, research suggests that racialized and immigrant youth of diverse backgrounds encounter an increased risk of social alienation and involvement with the criminal justice system and an increased risk of taking part in peer delinquency and gang violence.[10] Moreover, in regards to youth outcomes in the educational sphere, Light and Strayer's literature review reports that racial minorities are less likely than their White

---

[6]Bunch, C. (1997). The intolerable status quo: Violence against women and girls. *The Progress of Nations*, 1, 40-49.

[7]Abdo, N. (2006) Sexual Violence, Patriarchy and the State: Women in Israel. *Pakistan Journal of Women's Studies*, 13 (2), 39-63.

[8]Johnson, M. P. & Ferraro, K. J. (2000), Research on Domestic Violence in the 1990s: Making Distinctions. *Journal of Marriage and Family, 62*, 948–963.

[9]Brownridge, D. (2003). Male Partner Violence Against Aboriginal Women in Canada: An Empirical Analysis. *Journal of Interpersonal Violence, 18*(1), 65-83.

[10]Le, T. N., & Stockdale, G. (2008). Acculturative Dissonance, Ethnic Identity, and Youth Violence. Cultural Diversity & Ethnic *Minority Psychology, 14*(1), 1-9.

counterparts to succeed academically.[11] Researchers found that American youth from different racial groups (Blacks, Hispanics, and Asians) all described their limitations and goals in terms of racially sanctioned stereotypes even at a time as early as high school. Stereotypes acquired in high school link ethnic group membership to academic ability and other skills, many of which are compared to White students.[12]

Research suggests that Black children are more likely than children in the general population to be investigated for maltreatment cases in Canada.[13] Espinoza and Ek mention that race still contributes to longer sentences and harsher penalties, leading to juveniles being tried as adults.[14] Wright and Younts explain that African Americans are vastly overrepresented in all stages of the criminal justice system.[15] Additionally, when considering victimization studies, Blacks were frequently identified as offenders in crimes such as robbery, rape, or assault. This occurred despite the researchers reporting that in their study, there was, in fact, very little difference between the criminal behavior of Whites and Blacks.

Of specific concern is that, despite these issues, researchers explain that the differential rates are not solely attributed to race in and of itself. Freeman writes that in addition to societal and historical considerations, "economic status, irrespective of race, prevails as a more powerful surrogate of human conditions and circumstances."[16] Furthermore, rates of youth deviance, violence, or criminal involvement are more

---

[11]Light, A., & Strayer, W. (2002). From Bakke To Hopwood: Does Race Affect College Attendance and Completion? *Review of Economics & Statistics, 84*(1), 34-45.
[12]Kao, G. (2000). Group Images and Possible Selves Among Adolescents: Linking Stereotypes to Expectations by Race and Ethnicity. *Sociological Forum, 15*(3), 407-730.
[13]Lavergne, C., Dufour, S., Trocmé, N. & Larrivée, M.-C. (2008). Visible Minority, Aboriginal and Caucasians Children investigated by Canadian Child protective services. *Child Welfare, 87*(2), 59-76.
[14]Espinoza, R. K., & Ek, B. J. (2011). An Examination of Juveniles Being Tried As Adults: Influences of Ethnicity, Socioeconomic Status and Age of Defendant. *National Social Science Journal, 37*(1), 30-37.
[15]Wright, B. R. E., & Younts, C. W. (2009). Reconsidering the relationship between race and crime: Positive and negative predictors of crime among African American youth. Journal of Research in Crime and Delinquency, 46(3), 327-352.
[16]Freeman, H. (1991). Race, poverty, and cancer. *Journal of the National Cancer Institute, 83*, 526-527.

appropriately attributed to systemic discrimination, broken families, and poverty rather than specifically the race of the individual.[17][18][19]

Despite the evidence that these differential outcomes may be attributed to external influences rather than on some intrinsic deficiency based on race, the internalization of negative beliefs about one's identity can be damaging. Drawbacks to possessing socially influenced beliefs about one's racial inferiority are corroborated by Williams.[20]

The author explains that racial minority children can be affected by limiting beliefs about their race. He proceeds to mention that racial minority adults who live their lives in the context of a racist society are less likely to have comparable ratings of educational, socioeconomic, or even mortality rates to White adults.

Hence, we see the cyclic nature of these differential outcomes. Challenges are faced by racial minorities in health, relationships, childcare, and the criminal justice system. Mental health workers of multiple domains are thus likely to encounter diverse populations based on the high representations of these groups in the literature. This underlines the necessity of trained professionals to assist and support racially diverse children and their families.

When Did Race Start?

There is both a historical and present-day creation of race and culture to explain our perceptions of future encounters. The only way that you can justify the subjugation of others is through constant delegitimization. This is best illustrated by reading a dictionary. It's highly probable that if you go to the section that defines what "black" means, besides seeing my racial group, you will likely see things that are unpleasant such as dirty, soiled,

---

[17]Wright, B. R. E., & Younts, C. W. (2009). Reconsidering the relationship between race and crime: Positive and negative predictors of crime among African American youth. Journal of Research in Crime and Delinquency, 46(3), 327-352.
[18]Brownridge, D. (2008). Understanding the Elevated Risk of Partner Violence Against Aboriginal Women: A Comparison of Two Nationally Representative Surveys of Canada. Journal of Family Violence, 23(5), 353-367.
[19]Williams, D. R. (1999), Race, Socioeconomic Status, and Health: The Added Effects of Racism and Discrimination. Annals of the New York Academy of Sciences, 896, 173–188.
[20] Ibid.

condemnation, discredit, despair, or disaster.[21] In contrast, when we look up the definition of "white," we see a different story entirely. White can mean that something is free from blemishes, favorable, fortunate, pure, or innocent.[22] You will see this in any dictionary; this dichotomy between black and white is striking yet ever-present. Black and white are really just neutral colors, but our use of the terms breathes life into them.

A Huffington Post article[23] from a few years back caught my attention, explaining that one of the most influential people in the world was not Jesus (gasp) but instead was Carl Linneaus. Although this was definitely a typical media clickbait, it referred to an important article. Eom and colleagues[24] discussed an analysis of Wikipedia articles showing that most articles you read will have a slant toward being White men from Western countries after the 17th century. The actual article's discussion section critiques this while the Huffington Post article celebrates this. Although Wikipedia is not intentionally racist, there is a clear bias in who we generally see as being in possession of knowledge or significance in the world, and perhaps a bias in authorship.

Regardless of the bias of Wikipedia, Carl Linneaus is important. He was significant because he was one of the first and major proponents of the made-up concept of race. Another slight aside, Müller-Wille explains that part of the controversy with Linneaus is that, in his seminal text, he instructs the reader to "Know Thyself" and then dissects all human races into four different categories (and colors): white Europeans, red Americans, yellowish-brownish Asians, and black Africans.[25] Not only is he distorting the expression "Know Thyself" out of its focus on self-

---

[21]Black (n.d.) In *Merriam-Webster's collegiate dictionary*. https://www.merriam-webster.com/dictionary/black
[22]White (n.d.) In *Merriam-Webster's collegiate dictionary*. https://www.merriam-webster.com/dictionary/black
[23]Tamblyn, T. (2014, June 12). Wikipedia Reveals Most Influential Person In History, No It's Not Jesus. *The Huffington Post*. https://www.huffingtonpost.co.uk/2014/06/12/wikipedia-most-influential-person-jesus_n_5487516.html
[24]Eom, Y. H., Aragón, P., Laniado, D., Kaltenbrunner, A., Vigna, S., & Shepelyansky, D. L. (2015). Interactions of cultures and top people of Wikipedia from ranking of 24 language editions. *PloS one, 10*(3), e0114825.
[25]Müller-Wille, S. (2014). Linnaeus and the Four Corners of the World. In *The Cultural Politics of Blood, 1500–1900* (pp. 191-209). Palgrave Macmillan, London.

knowledge, an expression which, though few people know, was first recorded in Egyptian precepts on the Temple of Luxor and then culturally appropriated and arguably plagiarized by the Greek philosophers who we know and love.[26] It is not this that is problematic; it is that this racist (and largely inaccurate) categorization and pseudoscientific interpretation of all races was consistently used to prop up beliefs of racial hierarchies in which White people are more valued than others. Race has this as a function. The idea was not to follow the dictum of our Egyptian ancestors and focus inward. As a general concept, race was constructed and reconstructed for the purpose of outward conquest and subjugation.[27]

> ## Note:
>
> It is important to note that anti-Semitism should also be categorized as an early form of "race" based discrimination as this form of systemic oppression towards Jewish people may have started even prior to 300 BCE.[28] Additionally, the experiences of anti-Black racism also appear similar to casteism. Those most disadvantaged by India's caste system (e.g., the "untouchables," the Dalits) also face significant barriers toward upward mobility and severe violence based on their group's categorization.[29] The Indian caste system distinctions were created around approximately 1000 BCE.[30] There are, of course, other forms of discrimination as well. Systemic oppression in different societies predates European civilization, but the social construction *and* color-coding of groups is a relatively recent invention.

Who is Racialized?

Race creates a caste-based system that positions certain people to be granted privileges and others not. While we are all racialized, it is not

---

[26]James, G. G. (2013). Stolen legacy. Simon and Schuster.
[27]Rutherford, A. (2020). *How to Argue with a Racist: History, Science, Race and Reality.* Hachette UK.
[28] Johnson, P. (2003, October 12). The oldest form of racism. *The Telegraph.* www.telegraph.co.uk/culture/books/3604398/The-oldest-form-of-racism.html
[29] Dutt, T. (2020, September 17). Feeling Like an Outcast. *Foreign Policy.* https://foreignpolicy.com/2020/09/17/caste-book-india-dalit-outcast-wilkerson-review/
[30] OER Services. (n.d.) *The Caste System.* https://courses.lumenlearning.com/suny-hccc-worldcivilization/chapter/the-caste-system/

intended for White people to "have" a race as much as Black people. The concept of race is often not for White people, which explains why the term "racial minority" is more widely used than "the racial majority," purely because we are not supposed to target White people with such words. Words such as "ethnic" and "race" are supposed to refer to the out-group rather than the in-group. Hence, we can gain cultural competence about Indigenous people. We can take African studies, but you will not see Caucasian studies because Whiteness is the default and standard of our society. White people do not have a race like men do not have gender— the absence of this form of categorization grants the privilege of a lack of categorization and compartmentalization. You can be anything if you are White, except you most definitely are not Black.

What is the Function of Racism?

So then, understandably, the function of racism is two-fold: requiring an in-group and an out-group. The in-group is meant to benefit at the expense of the out-group. The active means of maintaining this benefit leads to the out-group being subjected to classification, dehumanization, and exploitation, while the in-group simply enjoys the benefits. In the absence of these stresses, the in-group has but to have the out-group be in a state of subjugation for there to be a passive benefit. When the time comes for solidifying or reinforcing subjugation, then the active benefit is realized not only by actions of the in-group but by beliefs about the out-group shared by both groups' membership. The detrimental effects are both active and passive. The two enemies then are not only the in-group perspective concerning the out-group but even the out-group's perspective on itself.

The "Identified Patient"

When we then discuss what the function of racism is, know that, just as if we were to talk about a family system, we have to see who in the system actually possesses power. Parents can, at times, request that a family therapist fix the child's problem and will be surprised when we invite the parents and siblings in for a session as well. In a family hierarchy, the child does not always have as much power—economically or physically, in both literal and figurative senses—when compared to the parent. So, the child's problem becomes a shared responsibility of all members of the system.

This idea of complementarity is important not only for family relationships but also in friendships, intimate relationships, businesses, and even international relations between countries. When we look at the "identified patient" who is seen as the problem, we must also look at who is part of their family. The identified patient did not start this way. Their problem could have been inherited by their family system. Assessing whom they communicate with on a regular basis can help us to explain why they have been identified as being the problem.

The Black-White Binary

In a White Supremacist society, you will see that "Black" must be the identified patient. Black is seen as childish, never mature. Black is problematic because of their dress, which is never proper. Black is unkempt because of their hair, which could never be straight. Black must be maintained as being the absolute worst; otherwise, White "could" be. Black must be bad for White to be good.

Black music must be bad so that we know that White music is proper. Black skin must be bad so that we know that White is more "fair." It is only "fair" that Whiteness is seen as ideal because deep down inside, there is an unconscious fear of not living up to myth-making expectations. White must be good because Black is bad. Because if Black were not bad, then White would no longer be perfect. This binary leaves very little room for interpretation. Hence, White supremacy is a game where everyone plays, and everyone loses. White cannot accept Black because White cannot *yet* accept its own imperfection and instead projects it unto its seeming opposite.

Any therapist would be a fool to categorize a teenager as "bad" because of their desire for self-expression. They would also be foolish to deem a child as the problem in an alcoholic household. We do not (except in oppressive cases, generally speaking) blame the woman who has been beaten by her abusive partner, so why do we blame the Africans for the siphoning of their natural resources? Why do we blame the homeless in a society that has billionaires? The function of racism is to excuse the moral failings of an imperfect society striving to project perfection. This lunacy must not continue.

IN SUMMARY

Race is a social construct that had specific and intentional reasons for its creation, none of which were for the benefit of those classified and bounded by its pseudoscientific nomenclature. It's a concept that started around the time of European colonialism, and its goals and use are related. It is a caste-based system that seeks to organize and structure our social order. A consequence of living in a White Supremacist social order is that Whiteness is seen as the default. All other variants are seen as "others." From a systems-based perspective, there is a function for maintaining anti-Black racism, differential treatment, and the other racial hierarchies based on this form of communication. It is designed to maintain a system where White is preferred, and others are tolerated. Systems theorists would see this system as oppressive not only for the victims who are targeted but also for the complete insecurity of those at the top of the social hierarchy. The extent to which the oppressed suffer is the extent to which the oppressors fear suffering. Anti-Black racism is primarily a White person's problem that ends up affecting Black people.

CHAPTER 2:

THE SOCIAL CONTEXT FOR SUFFERING

Fix the Identified Patient

"Well, will you be able to fix our son?" the father asked. "Since your child lives with you," I said, "we would also need to get an understanding of the home environment, how you all interact with one another, including how you and your husband react to one another."

Reluctance crept into the father's voice. He had not thought that his son's issues could be linked to their impending divorce. Nor had the father considered that his son's troubles and suspensions in school were a cry for help and a means of uniting both parents.

The man, holding back tears, blurted out, "I don't want to screw up his childhood like what happened in mine." The pain of childhood adversity was apparent. The intergenerational pattern of divorce originally experienced by the father was now affecting his son. Family therapy required the participation of the whole family so we could understand what was impacting each family member. We needed to take into account all parts of the system and not just the "identified patient."

The problem in the patient can sometimes be part of a legacy of disturbances. When working from a family systems perspective, the client is not the individual but the individual's family system. Our interventions have to consider the families we originate from and our unconscious patterns, which allow for the issues to replicate themselves through the generations.

The Systems Approach to Anti-Racism

Much like the example above, anti-racism is not an individual practice. Even if it can occur in individual, couple, family, or group therapy, we all exist in the context of interlocking systems. This chapter is dedicated to explaining the general foundational principles of anti-racist psychotherapy. Please note that any psychotherapy or clinical intervention is capable of having anti-racist aspects to it, and so this approach does not preclude other approaches from also being anti-racist. But an anti-racist psychotherapy is one that is systemic by its very nature and seeks to challenge and address functions of oppression at the source. The problem is not only what the client brings into the office, but what maintains the problem outside of the office.

Dr. Kendi explains in his book that it is necessary for us not just to look at the so-called racist or the so-called "racist" idea, but the racist policies and circumstances that precede them.[31] In this way, I share with Dr. Kendi an approach that is systemic in that it is inherently meant to target systems of operation. Such an approach may be more efficient and less prone to victim-blaming, which is what our clients and the general Black, Indigenous, and People of Color (BIPOC) community are most accustomed to. Certain aspects will be explained partially here and more in-depth later on. The key aspects to consider are the six Tenets of Critical Race Theory: Principles of Communication in Family systems, The Practice of Mindfulness, Young's Five Faces of Oppression, Multi-generational Transmission and Stress responses, The Adaptive Information Processing Model, and Memory re-consolidation.

---

[31]Kendi, I. X. (2019). *How to be an antiracist*. One World.

Critical Race Theory

Derrick Bell was a professor, an activist, and a human being who fought for the rights of millions of Americans. He was the first tenured Black law school professor in Harvard Law School,[32] a member of The National Association for the Advancement of Colored People (NAACP), and a leader in litigation for the desegregation of schools in America.[33] The perspective of critical race theory is controversial now but was even more so at the time that it was developed. Bell explained that critical race theory is not an approach that is deconstructive but rather redemptive.[34] In a context of understanding why Blacks are disadvantaged, we must have an understanding of the forces which maintain racism. It is explained that there are active forces to maintain homeostasis of Black inferiority and White supremacy.

Bell explains that this may be because any indication of Black superiority or success has throughout history been responded to with White outrage. Many of the race riots and lynchings in the United States were due to White-led violence, often in response to Black success or the fear that Blacks could potentially compete with Whites for resources, success, or even love. He adds that even in the most professional elite schools, there may be an unconscious preference for Black mediocrity.

Even if there are affirmative action policies (though we do not have them in my country), any BIPOC professional, myself included, has had to endure an initial acceptance from White students or professionals, only to be later targeted or disparaged when our performance exceeds what was initially seen as a charitable or merciful acceptance of a lower-tiered competitor.

---

[32]Dudziakm M. L. (2007, May 21). New Archive: The Derrick Bell Papers. *Blogger*. https://legalhistoryblog.blogspot.com/2007/05/new-archive-derrick-bell-papers.html

[33]Bell, D. A. (1976). Serving two masters: Integration ideals and client interests in school desegregation litigation. *The Yale Law Journal*, 85(4), 470-516.

[34]Hall, G. (2012, March 8). Derrick A. Bell: Who's Afraid of Critical Race Theory? *Blogger*. https://lawdawghall.blogspot.com/2012/03/derrick-bell-whos-afraid-of-critical.html

Bell explains this concept by citing another well-known critical race theorist, Richard Delgado, explaining that this psychological concept is more apt to be seen as cognitive dissonance. The former belief of inferiority opposes the current reality, and this is too much to bear. The corrective action is collective outrage and violence to level the playing field. As I see it, critical race theory is a means of explaining the "why" for systemic racism. It is clear that this perspective then sees racial injustice as being as American as apple pie. But since I am Canadian, it is also as Canadian as poutine, or maple syrup, maybe?

Mindfulness

When I conceptualize mindfulness, I am inspired by the perspectives of Vipassana meditative traditions. Vipassana meditation was popularized by Satya Narayan Goenka. While the approach was originally developed over two and a half millennia ago and is said to have been a means of liberation practiced by the Buddha, the approach and practice are secular.[35] When I conceptualize mindfulness, I will refer to the Eastern philosophies of being present-oriented, equanimous, and devoted toward the elimination of suffering, while still acknowledging that my use of these perspectives is both borrowed and interpreted to the best of my contemporary capacity and reality. Still, most meditators, regardless of their teachings, will appreciate the importance of diligence, sustained practice, and self-reflection. Here I include mindfulness as a tenet due to the need to recognize that any approach toward anti-racist psychotherapy must also consider the importance of centralizing the acknowledgment of suffering, the pursuit of inner wisdom, and the impassioned plea for more compassion to be brought into this world.

It is also important to note that these perspectives on mindfulness and meditation as being ways of coping with suffering are not new. Although widespread Western interest in some of these Eastern philosophies is quite recent, they may be somehow familiar to psychoanalysts in particular. Epstein makes various comparisons between Freudian thought and the ideas expressed in Buddhist perspectives.[36] The author explains that

---

[35]Hart, W. (2011). *The art of living: Vipassana meditation as taught by SN Goenka*. Pariyatti.
[36]Epstein, M. (1995). *Thoughts without a thinker*. New York: Basic Books.

Buddha was perhaps one of the first psychoanalysts of the world. Similar to psychoanalysis, the essence of Buddhist practice is to understand oneself in order to alleviate suffering. Epstein explains that one of the core questions in Buddhist practice is "who am I?" In attempting to answer this question, one must confront all aspects of oneself with honesty and clarity Epstein writes, "it is our fear at experiencing ourselves directly that creates suffering," yet paradoxically in Buddhist thought, that which causes suffering is also the means of release. It is ultimately the "sufferer's" relation to his or her thoughts that determines if the thoughts can be a vehicle toward either awakening or bondage. For this reason, then, our venture into the dangerous territory of race is both necessarily challenging and also the only way to solve the problem of racism.

Family Systems Theory and Communication

The Palo Alto Group was largely responsible for the initial development of family systems theory and practice. Although there was not a specific group because the members changed over time, this group typically refers to Gregory Bateson and his research associates or to Donald D. Jackson and his work at the Mental Research Institute.[37] The individuals involved came from a variety of backgrounds: Gregory Bateson was an anthropologist, Donald D. Jackson and John Weakland were pioneers in the field of family and brief therapies, and Jay Haley was known as a family therapy pioneer but is also well-known for introducing the work of Milton H. Erickson to the world. While there were others involved, these four were authors who wrote the seminal text of *Toward a theory of schizophrenia,* which revolutionized the field of family therapy and the scientific understanding of the role of communication in human systems.

It is necessary here to also mention Murray Bowen, who was another pioneer who conceptualized the family as a unit and brought in the

---

[37]Ray W. (2018) The Palo Alto Group. *In: Lebow J., Chambers A., Breunlin D. (eds) Encyclopedia of Couple and Family Therapy. Springer, Cham.* https://doi.org/10.1007/978-3-319-15877-8_596-1

importance of differentiation of self.[38] And I would be remiss if I did not mention other influential leaders in the field of family therapy, such as my personal favorites, Virginia Satir and Salvador Minuchin. Their later refinements to family therapy approaches—by bringing in experiential interventions, discussions of boundaries and self-esteem, as well as the capacity to express warmth and genuineness in their presentation and literary works—helps to inform the spirit of what guides even this piece of literature. These are three of the main therapists responsible for the conceptual shift leading us to consider that individuals are best understood from a family and a systemic context.[39] Of course, there are many others I could note, but a book can only have so many pages, and these are some of my main inspirations.

It is important, though, to highlight some of the findings of the Palo Alto group. They have made significant contributions to the field of family therapy and hence also to the continued study and development of anti-racist psychotherapy. There are certain principles in family therapy that changed psychotherapy in general because we are now not so much focused on the "why" of problems but more on the "how" or the "what" of the problem. Here are some concepts which are useful and necessary for additional study.

Symptoms

The family therapist typically sees symptoms in a family system as a response to a pathological context. A problematic symptom present in a system is capable of causing a disturbance in the entire system. Although it may be expressed in one person, there can be a benefit to its function to the entire system that it is a part of. Symptoms can be at the level of either an individual member of the system or can be the entire human system itself.

---

[38]Titelman, P. (Ed.). (2014). *Differentiation of self: Bowen family systems theory perspectives.* Routledge.
[39]Rockinson-Szapkiw, A. J., Payne, L. Z., & West, L. C. (2011). Leadership lessons from Salvador Minuchin. *The Family Journal*, 19(2), 191-197.

Meta-Communication

All forms of communication have two levels or functions: "report" or "command." If one member of a couple tells the other, "wash your hands, it's time for dinner," this would be the stated content of the message. Apart from the content, the message also conveys that the speaker is in charge. The underlying message of any communication is often implicit and not explicitly stated, at least in most instances.

Homeostasis

When a family structure faces a threat, the system will find a way of re-establishing stability. This does not mean that the stability is beneficial to all members of the system, but homeostasis entails maintenance of the structure of the family, hierarchies, privileges, and all. If there are two parents who are arguing with one another, and one child shows asymptomatic behavior, the symptom can be a form of uniting the parents through their concern. This preserves the equilibrium of two parents caring for a child, rather than two parents' conflict potentially altering the entire structure of the family.

Complementary and Symmetrical Relationships

Another important concept is that relationships can be symmetrical or complementary. Complementary relationships relate to differences that fit well together; one member of the family is passive, while another one is active. One member of the relationship is more extroverted, and the other is more introverted. Conversely, symmetrical relationships relate to more "equality," where one member's behavior can mirror the other. The danger with complementary relationships is that there can be domination or "unfairness," and symmetrical relationships can become adversarial or competitive.

Oppression and the Impact of Chronic Stress

Oppression is the act itself. Suffering can be interpreted as being not only the act that causes it but the residual damage from its occurrence. While all forms of suffering are damaging, some appear to leave "trauma" in the individual and scar our social orders. In Bessel van der Kolk's groundbreaking literary work, *The Body Keeps The Score*,[40] he explains similarly that it is not just the traumatic event as it occurred, but it is also the imprint that it leaves on the mind, body, and brain. Also, despite what we know about the findings of Felitti's Kaizer Permanente study on Adverse Childhood Experiences (ACEs)[41] and the later effects these would have on the developing child's later experience, our general society has either ignored or minimized the importance of the impact of trauma on all of us.

Studies on ACEs are very important because they show the cost of experiencing early traumatic events not only in childhood but, in some cases, even decades after the initial injury.[42] It is not only the events but the accumulation and variety of categories which lead to the worse effects. Felitti, Anda, and colleagues' landmark Kaiser Permanente study set the stage for some of the most major and significant findings in the field of trauma.[43] They found that there is a strong relationship between being exposed to childhood abuse or dysfunction in one's home and many risk factors that lead to premature mortality in adults. Also, the presence of one of these ACEs increases the chance of being exposed to another. And the greater the number of your ACEs, the more you experience negative health outcomes as you grow older. The findings have been replicated in many other studies. High numbers of recorded ACEs are associated with higher numbers of suicide attempts, more self-medication through nicotine and

---

[40]van der Kolk, B. A. (2015). *The body keeps the score: Brain, mind, and body in the healing of trauma*. Penguin Books.
[41]Felitti, V. J. (2009). Adverse childhood experiences and adult health. *Academic Pediatrics, 9*(3), 131-132.
[42]Chapman, D. P., Whitfield, C. L., Felitti, V. J., Dube, S. R., Edwards, V. J., & Anda, R. F. (2004). Adverse childhood experiences and the risk of depressive disorders in adulthood. *Journal of affective disorders, 82*(2), 217-225.
[43]Felitti, V. J., Anda, R. F., Nordenberg, D., Williamson, D. F., Spitz, A. M., Edwards, V., & Marks, J. S. (1998). Relationship of childhood abuse and household dysfunction to many of the leading causes of death in adults: The Adverse Childhood Experiences (ACE) Study. *American journal of preventive medicine, 14*(4), 245-258.

illicit drug use, higher chances of premature death, and a generally worse prognosis for both physical and mental health concerns.[44][45][46][47]

The impact of trauma, chronic stress, and how it impacts multiple generations will be discussed in a later chapter. But what is key to understand is that our stresses come in a variety of forms, and they have impacts that are above and beyond those normally discussed and thought of.

IN SUMMARY

The next chapter will complete the foundational concepts, but a summary of the above is as follows. Critical race theory posits that racism is a normal and natural part of the regular functioning of a system based on racial dichotomy and racial superiority/inferiority. This necessarily creates suffering. This is in line with conceptions of mindfulness in that suffering is a natural and essential part of our human condition. A perspective that focuses on the effects of systemic racism requires an understanding of the function of systems, meta-communication conveyed through explicit and implicit means, homeostasis, and dynamics of communication. And finally, different and varied forms of oppression contribute to adverse experiences leading to the transmission and exacerbation of suffering for all of us. These concepts provide the framework for the next chapters. Let us continue.

---

[44]Dube, S. R., Anda, R. F., Felitti, V. J., Chapman, D. P., Williamson, D. F., & Giles, W. H. (2001). Childhood abuse, household dysfunction, and the risk of attempted suicide throughout the life span: findings from the Adverse Childhood Experiences Study. *Jama*, *286*(24), 3089-3096.

[45]Anda, R. F., Croft, J. B., Felitti, V. J., Nordenberg, D., Giles, W. H., Williamson, D. F., & Giovino, G. A. (1999). Adverse childhood experiences and smoking during adolescence and adulthood. *Jama*, *282*(17), 1652-1658.

[46]Brown, D. W., Anda, R. F., Tiemeier, H., Felitti, V. J., Edwards, V. J., Croft, J. B., & Giles, W. H. (2009). Adverse childhood experiences and the risk of premature mortality. *American journal of preventive medicine*, *37*(5), 389-396.

[47]Felitti, V. J., Anda, R. F., Nordenberg, D., Williamson, D. F., Spitz, A. M., Edwards, V., & Marks, J. S. (1998). Relationship of childhood abuse and household dysfunction to many of the leading causes of death in adults: The Adverse Childhood Experiences (ACE) Study. *American journal of preventive medicine*, *14*(4), 245-258.

ANTI-RACIST PSYCHOTHERAPY

The Social Context of Suffering

The suffering of anti-Black racism is not an individual event, it occurs as part of a larger social system. It plays a role in our self-concept, our interpersonal relationships, and our lived experience in society. We are all part of this system.

Social Context

Critical Race Theory:
Necessitates confrontation with the social context of White supremacy.

Interacts with

Family Systems Theory

Individual Context

Mindfulnesss:
Necessitates confrontation with one's human experience of suffering.

Function of Symptoms

All symptoms in a system have a purpose and a function.

Meta-Communication

There are both explicit and implicit meanings to communication between all members.

Homeostasis

All systems seek to maintain stability and balance.

Taking into account all of the above:

The social context creates systematic oppression in order to maintain homeostasis in the context of White supremacy and Black suffering. This dynamic affects and influences all members of the social context.

CHAPTER 3:

THE MEMORY PROCESS OF SUFFERING

Converting

"So, what do you think?" I asked. The client started to walk towards the couch. He sat down and stared at the device in front of him. It was a smartphone-controlled, EMDR therapy apparatus with Bluetooth connectivity. The young man inspected it cautiously, as one might gaze at a predator that may unexpectedly jump at them. He was instructed to pick up the two pulsators, green triangular-shaped components, that alternatively vibrated under the therapist's control.

The pulsators were docked at the base of a long extending tube, connecting to a T-shaped futuristic light bar. On activating the light-bar from my smartphone, a blue light emerged from the light bar, alternately pacing from left to right, moving in perfect sync with the pulsators. As the light shone on the left side of the bar, it vibrated in the man's left hand; as the light traveled to the right side, it shook in his right.

He paused, turned his head toward me, and asked, "Are you gonna transform me into a Buddhist monk with this?"

We laughed. And then we proceeded to reprocess his traumatic memory.

It is a belief of mine that we must be willing to try something different for something different to happen. It may be necessary to rethink our understanding of how we look at our memories to see how they impact our present. This chapter will discuss the role that our memory systems play in our conceptions of trauma.

Reprocessing the Past

As change workers, healers, and psychological activists, we are all well-acquainted with the problems in our society. Adverse experiences at times seem to be the norm for our clients, but it does not have to be this way. There are ways of healing even the troubles which we see as most reluctant to change. Even for those which appear to be mediated from the past and maintained in the present, we now delve into certain concepts that are designed to resolve post-traumatic disorders and other psychological trauma.

Continuing from the previous chapter, I will now explain the core principles which explain how these changes take place. The previous chapter looked at the foundational principles relating to the system that allows and perpetuates trauma. Here we will discuss the processes that store trauma and a summary of mechanisms that assist in reprocessing and altering them.

A Deeper Understanding of Trauma

Isobel and Angus-Leppan provide a masterful summary of trauma.[48] They describe trauma as being both a key part of the etiology and worsening of mental health disorders. It manifests itself as an adverse experience in one's life. It is especially when these disruptions occur at key developmental moments, such as during childhood or adolescence, which leads to them having the most detrimental effects on a person's nervous system. The developing child has no other option than to view traumatic events as threats that imperil their very existence. The child learns from suffering. It then becomes imperative for the individual to develop means of coping, prioritizing survival over all else. This response

---

[48] Isobel, S., & Angus-Leppan, G. (2018). Neuro-reciprocity and vicarious trauma in psychiatrists. *Australasian Psychiatry, 26*(4), 388-390.

to a life-or-death scenario, while adaptive in the short term, becomes maladaptive in the long term. The drive to survive at all costs leads the traumatized individual toward patterns of hypervigilance, relational difficulties, and impairments to self-awareness. Trauma then becomes a problem of relationships: our relationship to our external environment becomes one of distrust; our relationship to our intrapsychic processes becomes one of insecurity. The child within us that experiences the difficulty suffers from the threat, the perception of the threat, and the memory that is etched into their consciousness.

The Adaptive Information Processing Model

The adaptive information processing model sets the foundational theory for Eye Movement Desensitization and Reprocessing (EMDR) therapy. EMDR therapy is a highly effective means of psychotherapy treatment that resolves traumatic material. EMDR therapy was developed by Francine Shapiro.[49] It was a model crafted in the late 1980s that evolved and was borne out of her own suffering; after being diagnosed with cancer, she diligently studied and sought out an approach that would be able to solve problems of the mind and body.[50] EMDR therapy is an approach that involves bilateral stimulation (BLS) alternating from the left side to the right side of the body while simultaneously attending to a "target" memory. Leeds explains that during the early period of 1989 to 1991, in order to address limitations observed for patients who had a history of eye problems or disability (e.g., blindness, eye strain, etc.), adaptations were made to include the use of bilateral stimulation beyond the use of just the eyes.[51] Bilateral stimulation in EMDR therapy now commonly includes the use of auditory tones or tactile stimulation either by remote or self-applied by the client.

---

[49]Shapiro, F. (2017). *Eye movement desensitization and reprocessing (EMDR) therapy: Basic principles, protocols, and procedures.* Guilford Publications.
[50]Luber, M., & Shapiro, F. (2009). Interview with Francine Shapiro: Historical overview, present issues, and future directions of EMDR. *Journal of EMDR Practice and Research,* 3(4), 217-231.
[51]Leeds, A. M. (2016). *A guide to the standard EMDR therapy protocols for clinicians, supervisors, and consultants.* Springer Publishing Company. 2nd edition. New York: Springer Publishing Company.

The Adaptive Information Processing (AIP) model sets the foundational theory for eye movement and desensitization. While the AIP is covered in depth by other authors, for the purposes of this book, we will list the three principles which are foundational for why EMDR therapy works and how change takes place from an information processing perspective. These principles are summarized by Leeds.

The AIP's Three Principles

Principle 1: All people have an intrinsic information processing system that has the capacity to recover from a state of disequilibrium and return to homeostasis. We all have a tendency to re-establish balance physiologically, emotionally, and cognitively.

Principle 2: Early experiences of suffering or chronic stress during the pivotal early developmental years affects the capacity for us to optimally operate this intrinsic capacity for recovery and restoration of homeostasis. When the disruption to the system is stressed beyond its limits, the experience becomes stored in a maladaptive form.

Principle 3: It is the combination of the structured EMDR therapy procedure and bilateral stimulation (hence the devices described in the opening paragraph) that reengages the AIP system. The resumption of information processing continues until it reaches a level that is idiosyncratically adaptive. If the client system has sufficient resources, an efficient resolution occurs. If the client lacks resources, further dysfunction persists. This necessitates the importance of preparation.

Leeds emphasizes that the third principle of the AIP is the capacity for the individual to heal itself and uses the metaphor of the surgeon. The surgeon operates on a patient in distress. The surgeon is thought to work on the body of the patient and remove the blockages to healing, but it is the body of the patient that allows wounds to heal. Leeds goes on to explain that we who use EMDR therapy are analogous to the midwife, in that we accompany the client in their journey and intervene only when necessary. We can only facilitate a process, not to prevent or accelerate, but to allow life to proceed at its natural pace.

Note:

What is important here is to understand that all people are always moving toward healing, if, and only if, there is a context and environment that allows and supports it. However, even the midwife is trained to intervene and save the life of the mother and child during a difficult birthing procedure. The therapist has a responsibility to intervene when it is necessary. EMDR therapy must balance the AIP principle of self-healing and the need for the clinician to guide the therapy process.

Explicit and Implicit Memory Systems

Our experiences of suffering, in some cases, are tied to stored memories of the initial act of oppression or injury. A summary of memory and which forms of memory we may need to engage with is necessary. Levine provides an excellent work relating to how trauma is stored in the body, and I seek to summarize his descriptions of trauma and memory here.[52] There are two main categories of memory we work with: explicit and implicit memory. The former is more conscious, the latter more unconscious.

Explicit memory is composed of two categories, declarative memory and episodic memory. Declarative memory relates to our laundry list of information: the "cold," hard facts. This form of memory allows us to tell stories that have a coherent structure with a beginning, a middle, and an end. This is what we are most conscious of and is used to communicate objective information to others.

Episodic memory is comparatively more "warm," autobiographical, vivid, and textured than declarative memory. Here we enter more into recounting more positive or negative feelings. Levine describes them as being more dreamlike or vague yet more interesting and spontaneous than declarative memory. They are less conscious than declarative memories

---

[52]Levine, P. A. (2015). *Trauma and memory: Brain and body in a search for the living past: A practical guide for understanding and working with traumatic memory*. North Atlantic Books.

but can still be recalled intentionally. Episodic memory provides the interface between the categories of explicit and implicit memories.

Implicit memories do not emerge consciously but manifest as urges, feelings, and actions. The two categories described by Levine are emotional memories and procedural memories. These two categories of memory can sometimes intermingle, rendering them difficult to delineate as being separate from one another.

Emotional memories are expressed by all mammals and are adaptive for survival. Certain experiences are "flagged" as important and felt as physical sensations. Our ability to feel anger, sadness, disgust, and fear, while they may not always be pleasant, are still as necessary for us to experience joy, pride, and love. These emotions are evolutionarily linked to certain "fixed action patterns," which would increase our chances of survival. They can often be the precursor to initiating a set of survival-based actions. In the field of trauma, however, the problem is that these emotional memories often trigger maladaptive actions, and here we visit procedural memories.

Procedural memories are the near-automatic impulses, actions, and body sensations that are generated from outside of awareness. These are the most unconscious forms of memory described out of the four. They are composed of learned motor actions (e.g., learning dancing steps, riding a bike, performing a Hadouken in a video game); emergency responses (e.g., fighting, fleeing, freezing up, bracing for impact); and the "organismic response tendencies" of approach/avoidance and attraction/repulsion (e.g., what makes us move toward a loving caregiver, what makes us exercise caution next to a dangerous precipice).

Note:

It is important to explain that there may be many other forms of unconscious memory categories that extend beyond the scope of our discussion. Additionally, there may not be any scientific means of truly establishing which forms of memory are "more unconscious" than others.

Because you guessed it, those forms of memory would be "unconscious." We have yet to completely decipher and understand the human brain.

While all memory categories are essential, therapists often focus on what happened (declarative) or the story behind it (episodic) during sessions. We do a disservice when we do not attempt to address the emotional drivers. Levine states, "indeed, persistent maladaptive procedural and emotional memories form the core mechanism that underlies all traumas, as well as many problematic social and relationship issues."[53]

The Process of Memory Reconsolidation

Ecker, Ticic, and Hulley cite extensive evidence that most of the symptoms and problems people address in therapy are generated by specific life learnings which, paradoxically, have adaptive intent and are carried outside of awareness in implicit and emotional and procedural memory networks.[54] Even though this form of knowledge is unconscious, these remnants of the past still impact our present behaviors, thoughts, urges, and actions. From unresolved issues in family of origin systems to attachment disruptions to external and internal stressors, there are a multitude of reasons why people need to go into therapy. The etiology of many issues is usually due to a set of circumstances and experiences that have left a mark on a person. From depression to eating disorders, many people can tell you when the problem started and how hard it is to get over it.

Emotional learning is stubborn and resistant to change. This is mainly because many of the approaches we use are "counteractive," meaning, for example, that we respond to a negative cognition with an opposing positive cognition to compete against it. We respond to emotional dysregulation with emotional regulation. We see the appearance of symptoms as being pathological or as a dysfunction of the person rather

---

[53] Levine, P. A. (2015). *Trauma and memory: Brain and body in a search for the living past: A practical guide for understanding and working with traumatic memory*. North Atlantic Books. 38.

[54] Ecker, B., Ticic, R., & Hulley, L. (2012). *Unlocking the emotional brain: Eliminating symptoms at their roots using memory reconsolidation*. Routledge.

than the normal functioning of the implicit memory systems. While counteractive approaches are, in some cases, best practices, as a rule, they are not the most effective forms of therapy.[55]

Up until the 1990s, many researchers regarded emotional learning as permanent. Psychological problems and symptoms were therefore viewed not only as psychopathology but also as "indelible" scars in a person's neurobiology. And it was not until the early 2000s that neuroscientists began to poke holes in the idea that our emotional learnings are our destiny. Supplementing the idea of a memory becoming initially consolidated, here we bring in the idea of reconsolidation.

The Therapeutic Reconsolidation Process

Ecker and colleagues explain the Therapeutic Reconsolidation Process as technique-independent, theory-independent, and composed of three main components: an accessing sequence, a transformation sequence, and a verification phase. The accessing sequence relates to identifying the presenting symptom (A), retrieving the emotional learning underlying the symptom (B), and then finding disconfirming knowledge (C), which is a vivid experience that is completely incompatible with the legitimacy of the emotional learning's model of reality. This last step can be a positive experience but need not be; it just needs to be capable of disconfirming and providing a mismatch of the emotional learning.

The transformational sequence involves the reactivation of this emotional learning (B), and the concurrent activation of the dis-confirming knowledge (C), pairing the two. Then the verification sequence involves determining if there is a lack of emotional activation of the target learning, a disappearance of the symptoms that had been generated by that unit of emotional learning, and a new permanent change in the client's perspective, belief, or actions.

The authors explain that in order for such transformational unlearning to take place, it cannot occur in an intellectual form but must occur in an experiential manner, although it could occur with the former. This is where the use of visualization comes in, in that the brain does not easily

---

[55]   Ibid.

distinguish between real and imagined experiences.

Consolidating the Foundational Principles
IN SUMMARY

Taking all of this into account, all people are part of interacting systems; we always exist in conjunction with a social system or external group. There is a bi-directional process and dynamic of communication that interfaces between one and another. Power impacts this, in that society often provides a unilateral top-down communication on the individual. Hence, the rules communicated by a social order place a greater role on each of us more than we individually place on the social order.

A perspective based on critical race theory sets the primacy of the experience of White supremacy as playing a role in our interpersonal and intrapsychic processes. While this experience of critical race theory posits that suffering and racism are ordinary, a perspective based on mindfulness allows us to consider that it is through the confrontation and acknowledgment of racism that we can interact with it and transmute it into wisdom.

Suffering is many times an echo of the initial pain we have experienced. Suffering is both the act of traumatization and the echo of one's memories of pain. The social processes that explain how this suffering impacts us are mediated by different forms of oppression. Still, we experience this in addition to the pain transferred to us, inherited from our forefathers and foremothers. The trauma of racism is not just limited to the past; it also involves the everyday "ordinariness" of microaggression and racial retraumatization.

The adaptive information processing model suggests that if individuals are given appropriate conditions, they are capable of mitigating suffering, healing from the constant retraumatization. It is natural to heal. Minor scrapes and scratches recover on their own. Healing from trauma is also possible and expected once appropriate space and context are provided. Approaches and techniques that facilitate memory reconsolidation are both time-efficient and highly effective for reprocessing the experience of suffering, the remnants of trauma, and are the key to solving the problem of racial trauma.

MEMORY PROCESS OF SUFFERING

Adverse experiences can lead to emotional, mental and physiological consequences. These experiences can be dysfunctionally stored in our memory. **Trauma** can become encoded in the body as a negative belief about ourselves. We all have the capability to reprocess pathogenic memories.

ADAPTIVE INFORMATION PROCESSING MODEL (AIP)*

PRINCIPLE 1

All people have the innate capability to recover

PRINCIPLE 2

Adversity is encoded in a maladaptive form in our memory system

PRINCIPLE 3

Dual attention to both the memory of the trauma and bilateral stimulation reengages the AIP

MEMORY SYSTEMS

EXPLICIT MEMORY

- Declarative memory: objective information and "cold" facts.

- Episodic memory: autobiographical and subjective information.

IMPLICIT MEMORY

- Emotional memory: "flags" important experiences, felt as physical sensations.

- Procedural memory: learned motor skills, approach/avoidance, survival reactions.

THERAPEUTIC RECONSOLIDATION PROCESS**

Accessing Sequence

- Identify the symptom.
- Retrieve emotional learning underlying the symptom.
- Present disconfirming knowledge.

Transformational Sequence

- Reactivate the emotional learning (B).
- Activate disconfirming knowledge (C) and prompt a mismatch with (B).
- Repeat pairing of (B) and (C).

Verification Phase

- Non-reactivation of emotions.
- Elimination of symptoms.
- Sustained change without the need for ongoing maintenance.

We can help ourselves to heal when we use the right approach.

*Leeds, A. M. (2016). *A guide to the standard EMDR therapy protocols for clinicians, supervisors, and consultants*. Springer Publishing Company. 2nd edition. New York: Springer Publishing Company.
**Ecker, B., Ticic, R., & Hulley, L. (2012). *Unlocking the emotional brain: Eliminating symptoms at their roots using memory reconsolidation*. Routledge.

PART TWO:
THE MENTAL HEALTH EFFECTS OF
SYSTEMIC RACISM

CHAPTER 4:

THE TENETS OF CRITICAL RACE THEORY

Classroom Chaos

There was whispering in the classroom. The students slammed their notebooks and spoke incessantly to one another during the class. They jeered and mocked the Middle Eastern professor.

"Yeah, yeah," they interrupted and mocked. The professor spoke on, explaining topics such as critical race theory and White privilege. These were terms that many of us, including the White students, had never heard before. Their whispering grew louder.

"Bullshit!" a young White lady screamed. The surrounding students cheered her on, parading around their desks, before unexpectedly leaving the classroom.

I was shocked, and the professor was stunned. The remaining students, of all races, looked around at each other, trying to understand what had transpired. Many of us had never before seen this level of outright disturbance during a class, much less in a university setting. I realized at the time that discussions of race could make even the primmest and most proper students regress to the level of bawling toddlers. This fragile reaction, this seemingly childish form of acting out, was somewhat familiar.

This also occurred in the therapy room. It was a rejection of surging feelings from the unconscious mind. Pushing these ideas of critical theory to the level of conscious awareness caused the students to immediately revolt and delegitimize the structure of the classroom.

I realized that this type of response toward a professor was not contingent on a person's level of education, degree, or social status. Resistance is to be expected before a substantial change can occur in psychotherapy. This pushback led me to believe, back then as it does now, that critical race theory was exactly the topic we needed to discuss.

The Six Tenets of Critical Race Theory

Critical Race Theory (CRT) explains the idea that many of the institutions that govern us are inherently racist, namely those of law and legal structures. Inequality is then maintained due to the maintenance of economic, social, and legal benefits for White people at the expense of these same rights for racial minorities. The intellectual origins of it stem from the 1960s but became more structured in the late 1980s.[56] A main figure in this framework is Derrick Albert Bell Jr. Among his many accomplishments, he was a prolific legal scholar and educator, having supervised over 300 cases on desegregation. He was also a pioneer, protestor, and an eccentric personality with unorthodox methods.[57] He is important because he was one of the prominent people who helped influence the tenets of CRT. We all need to be using the appropriate

[56] Encyclopaedia Britannica. (n.d.). Critical race theory: Additional Information. In *Encyclopaedia Britannica.com. Retrieved December 14, 2020 from* https://www.britannica.com/topic/critical-race-theory
[57] Bernstein, F. (2011, October 6). Derrick Bell, Law Professor and Rights Advocate, Dies at 80. *The New York Times.* https://www.nytimes.com/2011/10/06/us/derrick-bell-pioneering-harvard-law-professor-dies-at-80.html?pagewanted=all

vocabulary for us to know the rules of the game; the following will help us to navigate this game of anti-Black racism and White supremacy.

Critical race theory has six basic tenets (as summarized by Delgado & Stefancic).[58]

1. Racism is ordinary.
2. Racism serves a purpose.
3. Race is a social construction.
4. Differential racialization.
5. Intersectionality.
6. Unique voice of color.

Tenet 1: Racism Is Ordinary

We need to understand that racism is neither an abnormality nor an exception. The ordinariness of racism is such that the countries were founded on these ideals of racial violence. If the colonizers did not build our countries on the backs of Black people, if they did not treat the Natives as, how King[59] phrased it as "furniture" in the way they relocated and demarcated where and how they should exist, were it not for these oftentimes genocidal and massively violent events, then our suburbs would most likely be smaller. Our supermarkets would be just "markets." Our Walmarts would probably just be "marts."

And if we do remember that there were people who built this under the threat of violence, whipping, sexual violence, and kidnapping, then we can be inconvenienced. Slavery must be made to be seen as normal. We become desensitized to movies that show chattel slavery and see it as OK. For if we consider racism as wrong, then national pride becomes challenging.

Hence all of this to say, racism is normal and expected. It is not just the police officer; a perspective that explains that "Whiteness is superior to Blackness'" is necessary. All else is dysfunctional. As a Black man in a

---

[58] Delgado, R., & Stefancic, J. (2012). *Critical race theory: An introduction*. NYU Press.
[59] King, T. (2017). *The inconvenient Indian illustrated: A curious account of native people in North America*. Doubleday Canada.

White world, it is often only a matter of time during my daily operations that I will be confronted with an aspect of anti-Black racism. The news will report it to me, memes on my social media will remind me, I will be reminded of my Blackness and hence of my subordinate caste in a system that values White perspectives over Black experience.

Tenet 2: Racism Serves a Purpose

As mentioned earlier, racism is necessary for a system that suggests that there are racial hierarchies. So long as we ascribe different qualities, values, and worth to people depending on the reflection of their complexion, we will have the problem of racism. Racism is highly useful, though. Let us explore an important aspect of the critical race theory's explanation of its function.

Interest convergence. There is a convergence of interests that explain why racism has not been eliminated a long time ago. There is an intersection of class that comes into play here. The racial hierarchy benefits both rich White people and poorer White people. Rich White people are able to benefit from the labor of others. Basic economics highlights that there is a difference in power, depending on whether you are an employer or an employee.[60] There is an economic benefit for having it so that people with darker skin tones are relegated to certain employment prospects. It keeps things practical. It keeps things ordinary.

For those White people who do not have the unfair advantage of being in the place of an employer, there is a psychological benefit for anti-Black racism. Once more, because we are in a social order that suggests that it is preferred and desirable to be anything but Black, this will then be reflected in your media, in your daily operations, and even in your psychology. You can always rest assured that you are good as long as you are not a Black person.

As regular as racism is, we often find it in dating apps. Hutson and colleagues described how even in the realm of dating, the design of the apps and the behavior of the users often remind and reinforce the racial

---

[60] Wolff, R., & Barsamian, D. (2012). *Occupy the economy: Challenging capitalism*. City Lights Books.

hierarchies and implicit racial biases inherent in our social orders.[61] The researchers discussed how with the popular dating app OkCupid, White users are more likely than all other races to receive messages, go on dates, and are the least likely to date outside of their race. Two other important aspects of this are that heterosexual women, across the board, prefer White partners, and students in college are more likely to reject Black people, specifically Black women, as possible romantic partners. Racism may be ordinary, but it's not accidental—even in the online world there is a default preference and advantage if you just happen to click the button that says "White."

Tenet 3: Race Is a Social Construction

Critical race theorists would suggest that there is no biological or genetic basis for the concept of race. Race is a situational thing. Rutherford explains that, although variation in the appearance of people is normal, the concept of race was largely created as a backdrop for the intentions of European colonialism.[62] The idea of being a "pure" race is pseudoscientific and contradicts history. For the differences that groups of individuals have in terms of academic, sport, or any other competitive advantage, these cannot be based on the concept of race and much less genetics. Much of the variance of skin tones and complexions may have come about even before we left Africa and perhaps even before there were ever "White" people in the first place. He writes about race, "Our view of reality, so profoundly limited, has been co-opted into a deliberate political lie. We say 'black' when what we mean is 'recently descended from a continent that has more genetic diversity and pigmentation diversity than anywhere else on Earth.'" All people likely have Black ancestors. Racial purity is a myth; race is a social construct and not a scientific one.

What is also important is that not all White people were always "White." There are Irish, Italian, Greek, Hispanic, and many other individuals who may not have originally been seen as White when there

---

[61] Hutson, J. A., Taft, J. G., Barocas, S., & Levy, K. (2018). Debiasing desire: Addressing bias & discrimination on intimate platforms. *Proceedings of the ACM on Human-Computer Interaction, 2*(CSCW), 1-18.
[62] Rutherford, A. (2020). *How to Argue with a Racist: History, Science, Race and Reality*. Hachette UK.

may have been more of an emphasis on ethnicity than skin complexion. Although some immigrants were ostracized, stereotyped, and mistreated because they did not fit into what America or Canada wanted to call "American" or "Canadian," their mistreatment was very different from what Black people went through; indentured servitude was different from slavery.[6364]

As time passed, these very people who were previously disregarded because of their ethnicity eventually became "White," and many of the aforementioned ethnic groups benefit from White supremacy in a way that Blackness restricts. When enough people decide that someone is "White," they then become it.

Tenet 4: Differential Racialization

This concept is important mostly because it implies that people become racialized in a "different" way. Delgado and Stefancic explain that when looking at the appropriate worker class in the United States, there was a time when there was more of a need for Black labor then a need for Mexican and Japanese workers, and these needs changed depending on the needs of the society, the desires of the economy; these fickle and oftentimes contradictory criteria determine who is racialized and for what purpose.[65]

At the time of my parents' arrival in Canada, Black labor was required for housekeeping. But this fluctuates. While there were a number of reports about how Filipino-Canadians, in particular, have been over-represented in this field, as well as in other aide and assisted living fields of employment; the helping field, front line workers who have worked to prevent the public from contracting COVID-19, these people are largely

---

[63] Hogan, L. (2016, November 7). Two years of the 'Irish slaves' myth: racism, reductionism and the tradition of diminishing the transatlantic slave trade. *openDemocracy.* https://www.opendemocracy.net/en/beyond-trafficking-and-slavery/two-years-of-irish-slaves-myth-racism-reductionism-and-tradition-of-diminis/
[64] CBC. (2001). *Irish Immigration.* CBC. https://www.cbc.ca/history/EPCONTENTSE1EP8CH1PA4LE.html
[65] Delgado, R., & Stefancic, J. (2012). *Critical race theory: An introduction.* NYU Press.

people of color.[66]

Similarly, when we use terms such as people of color, we must be aware that our experience of being racial minorities are all different. The impact of 9/11 was a social and racial event in it that impacted North American society with a tragedy on home soil. Later ramifications appeared to occur relating to increased suspicion and questioning at the U.S./Canada border toward my Middle Eastern and Arab friends. Even with COVID-19, some of my Chinese friends reported instances of being confronted by "Karens" or White women who would weaponize White supremacy either by calling the authorities or assuming the posture of one; the list goes on. Race is not a uniform category. There is no monolith. We're all impacted by social factors differently, and non-White people can still be anti-Black racists.

Tenet 5: Intersectionality

This term was popularized by Kimberlé Crenshaw and, in her own words, intersectionality is:

> a lens, a prism, for seeing the way in which various forms of inequality often operate together and exacerbate each other. We tend to talk about race inequality as separate from inequality based on gender, class, sexuality, or immigrant status. What's often missing is how some people are subject to all of these, and the experience is not just the sum of its parts.[67]

The idea is that no one person has a single unitary identity. A White feminist could be Jewish. A Latinx person could be a republican. The experience of the White female therapist is different from the Black female therapist, which is different from the White-collar female client and the Blue-collar female client. There is no monolith.

---

[66] Luk, V. (2020, May 31). *How Filipino-Canadian care aides are disproportionately affected by the COVID-19 pandemic.* CBC. https://www.cbc.ca/news/canada/british-columbia/covid-19-filipino-care-aides-affected-1.5589603

[67] Steinmetz, K. (2020). She Coined the Term 'Intersectionality' Over 30 Years Ago. Here's What It Means to Her Today. *Time.* https://time.com/5786710/kimberle-crenshaw-intersectionality/

The status of being marginalized, meaning that you are shifted off to the margins and not put front and center like other groups, is a stress in itself. But it is unfair to say that all stresses are created equal. For example, being a woman means that there has to be a conscious understanding of biological sex. For many cis-gendered women, during a monthly cycle, there can be a reminder of one's gender. There is a specific time when a woman must become mindful of her engagements for that day or week. There are moments where she must plan for her menstrual period and do all kinds of things that cis-gendered men do not have to consider. As a man, I can be largely unconscious, relating to my gender. As a man by birth, much of the world sees my experience as the default, and it is by design.

For sexuality, a similar idea comes up, in that, for me, being a heterosexual is the default. If I want to access media that conforms to my idea of reality, it is fairly easy. "Coming out" has never been an issue for me. I can be mindless in my sexuality and still end up conforming to a general standard. It takes more effort to be a person who does not fall into the majority category because it is designed this way on purpose.

The simple fact is that being a White man carries a greater advantage than being a Black man. In a society founded on White supremacy, society is designed for White men at the expense of other men. Being a White man also means that there are advantages from being a White woman, even if they benefit from Whiteness. The more that we add color, poverty, sexual preference, immigration status, fluency in a European language and allow these characteristics to overlap, we recognize the importance of intersectionality. The more intersections between our identities that we have, the higher levels of complexity we have. While there could be stress due to my Blackness, misogynoir is even more detrimental. I am privileged in this way, and I benefit from the oppression of others. Similarly, a man from India benefits from my Blackness being more targeted and disadvantaged in both my country and in his. Other people being oppressed ends up taking the heat off of someone else's back. So there are differing levels of complexity beyond race.

Tenet 6: Unique Voice of Color

And, finally, we have the unique voice of color perspective. The general idea is this: because I am a Black person, I am able to see things that the White person does not see. Although not all Black people are qualified to talk on issues of race because not all skin folk are kinfolk, the general idea is that we need to have more unique voices to bring attention to things that others may not have on their radar.

We do not want to have it that the experts on feminism are men. We do not want it to be that the sole exposure we have to issues relating to sexuality only comes from mediums that are predominantly run by those who have mainstream, basic experiences. We need more LGBTQ voices. They can reveal to us ideas that those of us who do not fit into those categories can understand. We need people who have disabilities to tell us what freedom looks like. Only those who have personally navigated the chronic experiences of classism, xenophobia, ableism, homophobia, transphobia, and the countless other socially constructed obstacles are in the best position to inform us about them. We have multiple identities and come from a family of millions. When we restrict access to members of our family, we do not know what we have prevented.

IN SUMMARY

The five tenets of Critical Race Theory are essential in anti-racist psychotherapy. Racism is part of the everyday functioning of our societies. It occurs so often that anti-Black racism can be considered ordinary. Racism serves a purpose. So long as Black means that something is dark or imperfect, then White can always mean light or perfect.

There is both an economic and psychological benefit that goes to White people because of racism, at the unfortunate expense of Black people. Race was socially constructed and is reconstructed in the present. It satisfies the economic and political interests of specific groups who have more power than others. Racialization affects us all but affects us all differently. And though this book is mainly about race, let us not forget that those of us who are disabled, who are displaced, who suffer from trauma, those of us who do not fit as the most "perfect" are equally challenged in this system. And that each form of difference adds layers of complexity over each other form of difference.

And although there are many people of color, the focus in this book is on anti-Black racism. The fundamental problem lies in addressing the relationship between the extreme polarities of Black and White. Resolving this may also affect people between the spectrum; those who may also be caught up in the crossfire, but can sometimes still benefit from not being the main targets of this racial dichotomy.

It is important to note that Bell saw racism as a permanent fixture in American society.[68] This may be due in part to interest convergence and there being no great enough motivation to undo a structure that privileges the White global minority (despite being the default in some countries, White is still, after all, a minority group globally). I will not purport to know something greater than one of my inspirations. While he is a realist, I am admittedly an idealist. Because I often come across clients who believe that their trauma is permanent and still proceed to see improvements, I consider racism also a pathology that, with sufficient technology, we can reprocess. The Black Lives Matter protests of 2020, the global condemnation of anti-Black violence from people of all races, among other personal examples, instills this faith in me.

---

[68] Smith, A. (2012). Indigeneity, settler colonialism, white supremacy. *Racial formation in the twenty-first century, 66.*

CHAPTER 5:

THE GLASS CANNON - WHITE SUPREMACY

By Any Means Necessary

I shuffled forward as my dress pant legs brushed against each stair. Raising one leg after another in an overly dramatic fashion. I was 12 years old, wearing a suit that was oversized, climbing in front of a podium, and prepared to do a speech.

"The Ballot or the Bullet!" I chanted. Through the lens of my dollar-store imitation glasses, I tried as best as I could to channel one of my heroes at the time for my grade seven English class.

One of the greatest orators of our time was Malcolm X. Although I could not fully understand his message at the time, I later came to understand his significance and hoped that everyone else could know it as well. I would accomplish this by any means necessary, but the stage was set for it to occur during my English class Halloween oral presentation.

Malcolm X shared an idea that resonates with me even to this day: that White and Black are really just states of mind.[69] I would like to take some time to address this in the following two chapters, where I will discuss the concepts of White supremacy and Black suffering. In this chapter, we will discuss White supremacy, or the fallacy of White superiority, which purports that we are not all equal and that there is an inherent greater value in having a lighter skin complexion than a darker one.

This is a social construction among humans. Felines do not make this distinction. Humans gave the idea that Black cats brought bad luck. I do not think that our feline friends care about the color of one another's fur more than they concern themselves with dinner or sleep. But we are different. Because all people are categorized within the spectrum of "Black" and "White."

This chapter will consider a description of White supremacy, its functions, and its consequences.

Race as a State of Mind

I look at White as being a state of mind that a person can take up. It refers to one of dominance, perfection, power, and beauty. If we see it as a state of mind, it can make sense because anyone can take up the guise of being "White" and treat others as "Black." It is only that White people have a social contract that pushes them naturally in this direction. But rest assured, I have met some people who come from Sri Lanka, for instance, with darker skin than I have, who would hastily call themselves "Brown" before they would ever call themselves "Black," despite having complexions darker than my hair color. My South Asian friends are not the only ones. Many people have been known to buy skin bleaching creams in order to become something other than "Black." Instead, in India, they call it appearing "fair."[70] This is because the only other option is for life to become unfair.

---

[69] Malcolm, X. (2015). *The Autobiography of Malcolm X*. Ballantine Books.
[70] Diaz, T. (2020, June 26). *The Skin-Lightening Industry Is Facing A Long Overdue Reckoning*. Refinery29. https://www.refinery29.com/en-ca/2020/06/9885554/skin-lightening-cream-industry-changes-companies-unilever

This perspective of White being better than any other alternative is not just limited to White people; this occurs in intraracial interactions as well.[71] Nosek, Greenwald, and Banaji's study on associations of race to words such as "joy" and "failure" found that 88% of White people had a pro-White or anti-Black implicit bias.[72] While this alone may suggest why race is so influential in interracial countertransference, the study also revealed that minorities internalized similar biases. The authors explained that 48% of African Americans demonstrated a pro-White or anti-Black bias, and also that 36% of Arab Muslims demonstrated an anti-Muslim bias. Based on the pervasiveness of racial issues that exist in both interracial and intraracial encounters, there is much research that suggests that results such as these demonstrate the powerful effect of the larger social structure and cultural images in the average person's unconscious.[73]

Mays, Cochran, and Barnes provide a great summary of how deep discrimination resides in the nervous system.[74] In one section, in particular, they explain that there are many lab studies that demonstrate higher brain activity in the amygdala, the brain area which plays a key role in our experience of detecting threats when participants view Black faces as opposed to White faces. This was as true for White as it was for Black participants. Negative racial associations about Blacks are deeply entrenched and stored in implicit memory for both Black and White people. But why is all of this so deeply entrenched? I believe that White supremacy is more than a specific preference.

---

[71] Comas-Diaz L., & Jacobsen F. (1993). Ethnocultural transference and counter-transference in the therapeutic dyad. *American Journal of Orthopsychiatry, 61*(3), 392-402.

[72] Nosek, B. A., Greenwald, A. G., & Banaji, M. R. (2005). Understanding and using the Implicit Association Test II: Method variables and construct validity. *Personality and Social Psychology Bulletin, 31*,166–180.

[73] Tummala-Narra, P. (2007). Skin color and the therapeutic relationship. *Psychoanalytic Psychology, 24*(2), 255-270.

[74] Mays, V. M., Cochran, S. D., & Barnes, N. W. (2007). Race, race-based discrimination, and health outcomes among African Americans. *Annu. Rev. Psychol., 58*, 201-225.

Defining White Supremacy: Frances Cress Welsing

There are many different definitions for White supremacy. But first, I must include Frances Cress Welsing's definition:

> My current functional definition of racism (white supremacy) is as follows: the local and global power system structured and maintained by persons who classify themselves as white, whether consciously or subconsciously determined; this system consists of patterns of perception, logic, symbol formation, thought, speech, action and emotional response as conducted simultaneously in all areas of people activity (economics. education, entertainment, labor, law, politics, religion, sex and war). The ultimate purpose of the system is to prevent white genetic annihilation on Earth - a planet in which the overwhelming majority of people are classified as non-white (black, brown, red and yellow) by white-skinned people. All of the non-white people are genetically dominant (in terms of skin coloration) compared to the genetically recessive white-skinned people.[75]

Welsing's definition of racism is important for several reasons. She frames racism as being the same as White supremacy. She also situates White supremacy as being both a local and global system rather than just an individual form of discrimination, and there is a drive for genetic survival, which is included. As mentioned earlier, racial classifications are not based on genetics, but the issue of survival responses will become important for later chapters.

Defining White Supremacy: Andrea Smith

Aside from Welsing's definition, there are other ways of conceptualizing White supremacy that are necessary to explore. As Andrea Smith explains, White supremacy is made up of three different pillars, each intersecting and feeding into one and the other.[76] The first is

---

[75] Welsing, F. C. (1991). *The Isis (Yssis) papers.* Chicago, IL: Third World Press.
[76] Smith, A. (2012). Indigeneity, settler colonialism, white supremacy. *Racial formation in the twenty-first century, 66.*

anti-Black racism (also called "Slaveability") which keeps in place capitalism; genocide which connects to colonialism; and orientalism, which entrenches warfare. Anti-Black racism relates deeply to the idea of interest convergence and how the White/Black dichotomy is maintained in order to reinforce the commodification of people's bodies and the economic hierarchy (i.e., White dominates, Black subordinates); genocide, though referring to the struggles of Indigenous people, is explained as the need that not only must Indigenous people disappear, but that they must "always be" disappearing; and orientalism which gives some breathing room for those cultural groups outside of the Americas by seeing them as "exotic civilizations" while at the same time seeing them as a threat in need of eliminating. Smith warns that when we see White supremacy through a unilateral lens, we end up marginalizing different groups (specifically people who are indigenous to this country) or lumping everyone into the same category and minimizing differences.

Anti-Black Racism and Slaveability

White supremacy then is not only limited to the lack of preference for individuals; it is also a system that is meant to reinforce itself and replicate itself in actions both internal and external to the systems it is a part of. Slavery was problematic for Black people because they were treated as possessions, as tools for work. There was a domination-subjugation dynamic in that Blacks were intended to use their labor for the benefit of Whites. Blackness was then understood as a service toward an end, from child-rearing to crop farming. The labor and bodies of Black individuals were commodified, and this was entirely normalized in states and provinces. For centuries, for hundreds of years, the buying and selling of the Black body was inextricably linked to the economic system. The past of slavery is problematic because it is then undeniable, were it not for Black people, North America would not exist in its current form. Throughout the years, both the United States and Canada have been maintained by the delivery of essential services of people of color.

Whiteness then is meant to designate who provides orders to the other. Other authors have spoken about the psychological consequences of this setup.[77] Taking this into account as a state of mind, depending on your "Whiteness," how well you speak, how well you dress, where you live, the institutions you are a part of, you can either be or look more "White" than the next man. Because they are created by White people, many academic institutions are also created for White people, which ends up creating White people. This occurs irrespective of one's race. It is common for many second-generation immigrant or Indigenous children to give me an anglicized name to call them by so that they do not go through the shame of hearing their name butchered and mispronounced. Being White means being accepted as being the default. It also suggests humanness as opposed to objectification—or having one's existence based on providing a "service" for another's goal.

White Supremacy and Canadian History

The impact of settler colonialism is similar yet different from the racial aspects of discrimination. No other group of people in North America has been through the extent of state-sanctioned violence and disenfranchisement than Native individuals. Canada had a national policy of assimilation which in some ways was even more aggressive than the United States. This was done through a federal piece of legislation called the Indian Act.

I must take a moment to discuss the one-time head of the Department of Indian Affairs named Duncan Campbell Scott. He is known for saying the following:

> I want to get rid of the Indian problem. I do not think as a matter of fact, that the country ought to continuously protect a class of people who are able to stand alone... Our objective is to continue until there is not a single Indian in Canada that has not been absorbed into the body politic and there is no Indian question, and no Indian Department, that is the whole object of this Bill.[78]

Only recently has the Canadian government acknowledged that having people like that working for it and adopting policies that involved

---

[77] Grier, W. H., & Cobbs, P. M. (2000). *Black rage*. Wipf and Stock Publishers.
[78] National Archives of Canada, Record Group 10, vol. 6810, file 470-2-3, vol. 7, 55 (L-3) and 63 (N-3).

the residential school system amounted to genocidal practice. It is not only the scale of the violence, but it is the lack of any real mention of it. Smith explains that, on some level, it is as if the colonization was seen to have taken place in the past. While the arrival of the colonizers was an event that had a beginning and an end, the process of colonization is a present and continuing practice. The appropriation of Indigenous people's cultural identity, the violation of treaties, and the destruction of the environment continue to this day.

Orientalism and War

Smith's usage of the word "Orientalism" comes from Edward Said's groundbreaking book of the same title, but here Smith refers to the idea that anyone who is from an external "civilization," whether naturalized citizen or not, may also constitute as being a "foreign threat." This tendency is not just limited to Americans; globally, there has been an embrace of political groups that prioritize maintaining the homogeneity of a given country and opposing the idea of accepting immigrants or refugees. Smith explains that for the United States to keep the momentum of endless wars, it must also protect and divert criticism from slavery and colonization. For White supremacy to maintain itself, the countries which espouse elements of it must always be at war. It does not matter if the war involves a foreign threat or if the threat is within its own body-politic because you can always be an American and still be un-American.

In January of 2020, it was reported that a quarter of Americans have never experienced a time of peace.[79] There is an interesting statistic regarding talking about war. Based on Wikipedia entries, different individuals managed to calculate that the United States has been at war for 222 out of 239 years of its existence, meaning it has been at war for 93%

---

[79] Bump, P. (2020, January 8). Nearly a quarter of Americans have never experienced the U.S. in a time of peace. *The Washington Post*.
https://www.washingtonpost.com/politics/2020/01/08/nearly-quarter-americans-have-never-experienced-us-time-peace/

of its existence. This has been debated extensively online.[80][81]

The Consequences of Whiteness

In any case, people have long debated the role of war, racism, and genocide. What I argue is that each of these three categories represents an interlocked form of concomitant forms of winners and losers, violators and victims, oppressors and oppressed. In the term White supremacy, we see both the function and association drawn and revealed that Whiteness equals victory. This carries itself out in all categories and instances which involve an individual in a social system. Even if the individual is themselves alone, Whiteness must denote victory at all costs, even at the cost of the individual themselves.

A society that values one group over another and within its own make-up, intentionally creates in-groups and out-groups for subordination, cannot sustain itself. The detrimental effects of out-group subordination are balanced by the need of the in-group to maintain appearances and status. Hence not only are those who are in the out-group on the receiving end of this violent dynamic, but even members of the in-group suffer from the pressure to maintain it.

White supremacy is the game that everyone plays, and everyone loses.

Suicide Among White People

White people have to live up to a myth that targets them in terrible ways. Ivey-Stephenson explains that between 2000-2015 there were consistently higher levels of suicide among White subjects of all ages compared to Black subjects.[82] In a 15-year period, Black people were listed as completing suicides about 30,000 times. This was in comparison

---

[80] Shah, S. (2020). The US Has Been at war 225 out of 243 years since 1776. *The News International.* https://www.thenews.com.pk/print/595752-the-us-has-been-at-war-225-out-of-243-years-since-1776

[81] Charpentier, A. (2017, March 19). The U.S. Has Been At War 222 Out of 239 Years. *Freakonometrics, Hypotheses.org.* https://freakonometrics.hypotheses.org/50473

[82] Ivey-Stephenson, A. Z., Crosby, A. E., Jack, S. P., Haileyesus, T., & Kresnow-Sedacca, M. J. (2017). Suicide trends among and within urbanization levels by sex, race/ethnicity, age group, and mechanism of death—United States, 2001–2015. *MMWR Surveillance Summaries, 66*(18), 1.

to White people's completed suicides counting up to more than 450,000. Rates per 100,000 of the population came out to White people at 16.71 compared to Blacks at 6.35. Of White people who completed suicide, men generally have higher rates than women. Although White men are often seen as being most privileged as being the default "race" and "gender," why could there still be this disparity?

Dr. Canetto made a presentation explaining that older White men were most susceptible to committing suicide than any other racial or age group.[83] She explained that there is some intersection between masculinity, a social acceptance of suicide for this group, and a cultural script that enables suicide as a viable option. This cultural script is not universal in all countries; it is mainly a problem of the Western world, Europeans included. Interestingly, when a White man ages, he is also becoming disabled in some way, shape, or form. Could this move toward becoming a so-called "marginalized" individual be a worse fate than death?

Opioid Abuse and White Americans

Similarly, Alexander and colleagues also explain that there is a similar disparity that was observed between 2000-2015 as well.[84] Although both groups have been seeing increases over time, there is a higher rate of opioid-related deaths in White populations than in Black. They explain that much of this fatal increase may be due to the mixture of drugs such as fentanyl and heroin. But with regards to the opioid death rates, the authors explain that in 2000, the death rates were similar:

> By 2005 the death rate for the white population was 1.6 times that of the black population, with this ratio peaking at 2.4 in 2010 ... The latest data, from 2015, indicate the opioid death rate for the white population is around 12.5 deaths per 100,000 people, almost double that of the black population. Over the period 2010-2015, the death rate increased by 51 per cent for the white population

---

[83] Canetto, S. S. (2017). Suicide: Why are older men so vulnerable?. *Men and Masculinities, 20*(1), 49-70.
[84] Alexander, M., Barbieri, M., & Kiang, M. (2017). Opioid deaths by race in the United States, 2000–2015. *OSF*
Retrieved December 2020 from https://osf.io/preprints/socarxiv/jm38s/download

and 87 per cent for the black population.[85]

While opioid-related deaths are becoming a worse crisis for us all, there is still this disproportionate impact on White people and communities as a whole. Also worth noting is that both Ivey-Stephenson and Alexander's studies demonstrate that rural White Americans are hit hardest by both suicide and addiction.

Dr. Gabor Maté sees addiction as behavior that adheres to a short-term craving while keeping up longer-term negative consequences.[86] He was also at the forefront of seeing trauma as an important precursor to maintaining an addiction. When we discuss addictions, it is important for us to know that there is almost always a function to the drug. A person is only taking a specific drug mainly because there is a purpose for it. In this case, then, the addict who uses a pain killer could be trying to suppress pain. It does not necessarily need to be an actual pain but even emotional pain. For such a large number of people to self-medicate with such a lethal dose of anesthesia, we must consider that there are significant amounts of emotional pain carried within the White body.

Body Image and Whiteness

And for eating disorders, numerous researchers have found that anorexia nervosa appears to be a gendered disorder that affects mainly female-identified patients,[87] and there are some indicators that more young boys are starting to get it as well.[88] Anorexia is a very dangerous and challenging disorder to treat, involving a multi-disciplinary team of nutritionists, pediatricians, psychiatrists, and other mental health professionals. In their review of the literature, Arcelus and colleagues explained that the lifetime risk for developing anorexia was between 0.3% and 1.0% of the population, approximately only 46% of patients fully recover and that 20% of patients remain in the more chronically ill, or

---

[85] Alexander, Barbieri, & Kiang, 2017, pp.2-3

[86] Maté, G. (2008). *In the realm of hungry ghosts: Close encounters with addiction.* Random House Digital, Inc.

[87] Lock, J., & Le Grange, D. (2015a). *Help your teenager beat an eating disorder.* Guilford Publications.

[88] Lock, J., & Le Grange, D. (2015b). *Treatment manual for anorexia nervosa: A family-based approach.* Guilford Publications.

treatment-resistant category.[89] They also found that, while generally there is a higher mortality risk for those who have eating disorders, anorexia nervosa is generally more fatal than bulimia nervosa, for example. Generally, patients with eating disorders had higher mortality rates than other psychiatric disorders such as schizophrenia, bipolar disorder, and unipolar disorder.

While it was not as easy to find race data on disparities for anorexia nervosa prevalence, Gordon and colleagues found that while all American women are exposed to the United States' body image ideal of thinness, not all racial groups respond to it the same way.[90] In their study, the researchers found that White female participants were shown to have greater levels of body dissatisfaction than their Black and Latina racial counterparts. This is in part due to differing levels of the ethnic body ideal between groups. But what they did find is that Black and Latina women who had higher levels of acculturative stress or who felt pressure to fit in or assimilate to mainstream White culture would have higher levels of body dissatisfaction and eating disorder symptoms. While they explained that their study needed replication, in their research, acculturative stress would lead Black women to move toward bulimic behaviors while Latina women would be driven to attempt to become thinner. While this is a maladaptive means of managing stress, the authors cited that having positive views of the values of one's culture of origin may be a mitigating factor in reducing the most damaging effects of eating disorders.

The White Minority

While there may be a confluence of different aspects that may contribute to this drive of White supremacy, I believe there is one that is also important to consider. The United States Census in 2018 reported that by 2060 the "non-Hispanic White alone" population is expected to shrink

---

[89] Arcelus, J., Mitchell, A. J., Wales, J., & Nielsen, S. (2011). Mortality rates in patients with anorexia nervosa and other eating disorders: a meta-analysis of 36 studies. *Archives of general psychiatry, 68*(7), 724-731.
[90] Gordon, K. H., Castro, Y., Sitnikov, L., & Holm-Denoma, J. M. (2010). Cultural body shape
ideals and eating disorder symptoms among White, Latina, and Black college women. *Cultural Diversity and Ethnic Minority Psychology, 16*(2), 135.

by about 20 million, going down to 179 million.[91] This shrinkage is due to lower birth rates and higher death rates. But the "White alone" population, which includes Hispanic, is projected to grow 20 million from today to 275 million. Additionally, what they call the "Two or More Races" category is projected to be the fastest-growing group over the next few decades in part due to natural increases and immigration.

The violence of White supremacy then can be perceived as being a response to much of the above. Despite a system that promises victory, there are diminishing numbers. This will not necessarily stop White supremacy because you only need the power to be concentrated in the hands of the few, but North America will fundamentally change when White people can no longer call themselves the "majority" or "dominant" or "normal" members of society. It is this fear of being replaced, which in part drives the urgency and survival responses that drive the policies and practices of White supremacy at all costs.

IN SUMMARY

White supremacy is multi-faceted but is largely based on a structure of privilege and dominance. Whiteness is valued and must be valued by all members of society in order for the rule to be maintained and followed. The three pillars of White supremacy are anti-Black racism, genocide, and managing foreign threats. The concepts of in-group and out-groups are helpful for understanding racism but may be insufficient to fully justify the disproportionate level of maintaining racial injustice to this extent. There may be an aspect of collective trauma that is either intentionally buried or unintentionally neglected in our national dialogue. But what is clear is that the higher levels of suicide, opioid overdose, and eating disorder/body image issues may represent that the glass cannon of White supremacy is untenable. Not only is it untenable for those who call themselves White, but also for my allies who "happen" to be White and

---

[91] United States Census Bureau. (2018, September 6). *Older People Projected to Outnumber Children for First Time in U.S. History.*
https://www.census.gov/newsroom/press-releases/2018/cb18-41-population-projections.html

recognize the unfairness in the racial imbalance.

A COMMENT ON WHITE SUPREMACY:

I have been asked to comment on the events of January 2021 and I offer my explanation here. Thousands of White rioters stormed the United States Capitol building. It was violent. Some people lost their lives. The mob broke through police barriers, destroyed property, wreaked havoc through the halls and sought to disrupt a peaceful transfer of power to the incoming presidential administration. While some news pundits blamed it on the then president at that time, others were confused, believing that it seemingly came out of nowhere. I was not confused by this. It looked very familiar to me.

As a therapist, if I were able to have a country as a client, say the United States (or Canada), who in its past, in its early formative years, embarked on a crusade of exploitation for material gain, sought the extermination of Indigenous people, engaged in forced enslavement, and proceeded to do this for centuries, this client would likely be disturbed in the present. Violence on such a protracted and drawn out scale cannot occur without both a consequence to the victim and the oppressor. For my everyday clients who have suffered significant adverse childhood experiences and chronic stress during key developmental periods, whether ritualized abuse or even grave crimes against others, it is not possible for them to sit idly in my office without some kind of twitch, tic, or physical disturbance. I assume that the country itself, as a client, would also present in a similar fashion, likely accompanied by some sort of persistent mental illness and a compulsion towards employing a deep psychological suppression to their past identity or identities. The memory of past trauma can in some cases be blanketed out by a psychological process called dissociation.

What we saw during this riot was not unusual. Our countries, and their people, are deeply traumatized. People who have been through complex forms of trauma sometimes have flashbacks. Sometimes our past trauma is not fully processed which is why some rioters carried confederate flags. Many people have sustained injuries in the past that are still unresolved, conveniently ignored, and there is no plan for sincere apology from the offending party (as that would imply guilt or, worse yet, weakness). When we look at these seemingly aberrant events through the lens of trauma and from a family systems perspective, we gain different explanations for the dissociative identities of our countries. The denial of racism, the whitewashing of history, these among others are convenient methods of dissociating from the violent events that permitted our countries to exist in the first place. Flashbacks are often unexpected, and at times inexplicable, especially when we have tried hard to forget the trauma that triggered them in the first place.

WHITE SUPREMACY

There are multiple definitions, but White supremacy (racism) is always a multi-faceted and systemic issue. It is designed to ensure complete and persistent victory.

FRANCES CRESS WELSING'S DEFINITION OF WHITE SUPREMACY*

Structured and maintained by White people

Systemic Racism
It is a local and global power system

Influences Patterns of Perception
Conveyed through: logic, symbols, communication (speech/action/emotion)

Conducted Through
Economics, education, entertainment, labor, law, politics, religion, sex, and war

Purpose
To prevent the genetic annihilation of White People

ANDREA SMITH'S THREE PILLARS OF WHITE SUPREMACY**

Not a single issue, but separate and distinct interrelated logics

Slaveability/Anti-Black racism
Anchors capitalism

- Applies a racial hierarchy.
- People become commodities.

Genocide
Anchors colonialism

- Native peoples must "always" be disappearing.
- Non-Native people then rightfully inherit land, resources, and culture.

Orientalism
Anchors war

- The West is seen as superior to the inferior Orient.
- Foreigners are seen as permanent threats, hence we are at a continuous state of war.

HOWEVER, IT IS A GLASS CANNON

Though powerful, it simultaneously harms those who benefit...

Mental health consequences of White Supremacy

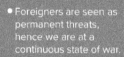

↑ Prevalence of eating disorders

↑ Rates of opioid abuse

↑ Rates of suicide

*Welsing, F. C. (1991). *The Isis (Yssis) papers*. Chicago, IL: Third World Press.
**Smith, A. (2012). Indigeneity, settler colonialism, white supremacy. *Racial formation in the twenty-first century*, 66.

CHAPTER 6:

MAINTAINING SOCIAL DEFEAT – BLACK SUFFERING

Security Check

I remember my third week at the internship. Walking into the building and sniffing the fresh smell of "hospital." My ID card swayed back and forth, mimicking the pace of my brisk movements. I moved through the lobby, greeting the security guard. He was Black, just like me. Because all of the security guards were always Black.

I waved to him, "Mornin' sir!" He was an older man who was hard of hearing. Perhaps he forgot my name. But remembering my name was not as important as referring to me as "son."

"Morning, son," he responded with a genuine smile.

We smiled back at each other for a moment. We both saw our Blackness mirrored in the other. We found solace in seeing the reflection of one another's mutual shared sense of humanity.

With my ID card in hand, I approached the front desk where I would log my attendance and write that I was present. My desire to complete this task was interrupted by a large White woman who shuffled ahead of me, blocking my entry. She sneered and stood her ground. It was her territory to protect, this coveted area littered with dusty files and old manuals.

She immediately stepped into my personal space and yanked my ID card forward, peering at it through her red-colored glasses. She uttered the words, "Oh, OK, you work here," and then cleared the path.

I felt violated. It was not violence, but I felt the impact.

I looked toward the old man, and he was busy greeting the patients and family members who walked through the entrance. Did he see what happened? Did anyone else see what just happened? I felt ashamed. Even though this woman had seen me enter the building several times before, she would see an intern as a threat. Or maybe it was something else; she would see me as a Black threat.

I retreated into myself, knowing that I had been outed. I was Black once again. She was White once and for all. Her microaggression was a display of status, dominance, and labeling who was the boss around here. She returned to her secretary's desk across from the entrance. Her job was complete.

I held my head down as I passed her. I could feel the old man cry despite his smile.

Unfortunately, these experiences of microaggression are common for people who are considered part of an out-group. This chapter will describe some of the social functions and consequences of Black suffering and its relationship to trauma.

Experiencing Blackness

Malcolm X explained that White is a state of mind. And Black is a state of mind, too. But it is a label that is not only given at one time in history; it is repeatedly given through media, popular culture, and micro-interactions that reinforce and remind the Black person that they are different. I am Black because someone made me Black. But my experience of Blackness is entirely subjective.

An individual's perception of the world can, at times, be a consequence of the oppression they have experienced. For this reason, it is important for therapists of all backgrounds to identify with the worldview of a client in a way that does not further marginalize them. Black clients and their families may present as suspicious upon entering "White institutions"[92] with the expectation that a White social worker, psychologist, or other professional may reinforce the alienation and condemnation that they have come to expect from society. Connell states that many racially diverse clients cite experiencing prejudice by clinicians as a reason for not returning to therapy.[93] This necessitates an approach that acknowledges the lived experiences of racially diverse clientele with empathic consideration of their unique daily struggles.

While the dictionary and other texts will establish Black as bad because White is good, I have a different perspective. If White is in fact, a state of mind, then Black must be too. Blackness does not have to be bad; it only becomes bad if you are White. Black is then the antithesis of White. If White supremacy is based on the foundation of domination, subjugation, and the drive toward perfection, then the idea of Black is that of resistance, the drive toward humanity despite demonization. Black is imperfect if White is perfect. And, like alternating and imperfect chords, the struggle of race becomes the soundtrack to the Black person's life, reverberating through an auditorium of Whiteness.

Internalized Oppression and Inferiorization

For White supremacy to exist, though, the echoes of Black suffering become necessary. Even if it is unlikely, it must occur at all costs. In the

---

[92] Boyd, F. N. (1987). The Contributions of Family Therapy Models to The Treatment of Black
Families. *Psychotherapy: Theory, Research, Practice, Training*, 24(3), 621-629.
[93] Connell, C. (2010). Multicultural Perspectives and Considerations within Structural Family
Therapy: The Premises of Structure, Subsystems and Boundaries. *InSight: Rivier Academic
Journal*, 6(2), 1-6.

absence of direct oppression, the Black person must believe that they are inferior. It is necessary to discuss internalized oppression here. Internalized oppression encompasses inferiorization. Inferiorization represents the internalizing of negative beliefs and conceptions about one's own culture or group. Internalized oppression "also encompasses behaviors (discursive practices) that are self-harming and contribute to one's own oppression."[94] An example of inferiorization could be a Black teenager who would come to believe that he is valued less than a White man, hence limiting his own self-concept and aspirations.

An example of internalized oppression would involve this same teenager accepting this socially instilled conception and adopting maladaptive lifestyles (through gang membership or drug abuse, for example), which would further reduce his opportunities and, in a way, seek to validate his and society's racist belief of inferiority. Thus, an endless cycle of self-destruction and external invalidation ensues.

I use the above example because this is a common stereotype, almost to be expected of Black people. Stereotypes are oversimplifications and inflexible attributions put onto large groups of people which are usually disparaging.[95] The repetition of stereotypes in culture allows for people to believe them.

Social Defeat

Dulka and colleagues describe, in rodent studies, that the concept of social defeat is used to model stress responses in humans.[96] The general idea is that if a rodent is placed into a situation where they suffer repeated attacks and intimidation from a rodent that is in its rightful territory, the so-called "defeated" rodents will have one of two responses—they will behave in a way that resembles either "defeat" or "resistance". In their

---

[94] Mullaly, B. (2010a). *Internalized Oppression and Domination. Challenging Oppression*
and *Confronting Privilege* (160-187). Don Mills, ON: Oxford University Press.
[95] Mullaly, B. (2010b). *Oppression at the Cultural Level. Challenging Oppression and Confronting Privilege* (93-125). Don Mills, ON: Oxford University Press.
[96] Dulka, B. N., Lynch III, J. F., Latsko, M. S., Mulvany, J. L., & Jasnow, A. M. (2015). Phenotypic responses to social defeat are associated with differences in cued and contextual fear discrimination. *Behavioural processes, 118*, 115-122.

literature review, the authors explain that the defeated response resembles listlessness, depression, anxiety, and an increased reaction to the Hypothalamic Pituitary Adrenal (HPA) axis. The resistant response does not include the depressive reaction, but they still had increased anxiety and high levels of HPA axis reactivity. The authors explained that mild and repetitive experiences of defeat can create a vulnerability to fear in both cases and a decreased capacity to feel safe even in neutral or different environments.

In a similar way that Indigenous people must always be "disappearing,"[97] Black people must always be "defeated." Black people must always be young, never old. Black actors must be criminals, never heroes. It is essential that videos show dead Black bodies, and you will not recall the last time you saw a dead White body on your social media, but you may have an easier time recalling depictions of Black or Brown victims. There needs to be a constant reminder that Black people suffer, which legitimizes why they cannot have nice things.

Shepherd reached a similar conclusion. Racism, as it exists, increases the risk of a person experiencing psychological illnesses.[98] Through overt and covert acts of oppression, through the negative portrayals of Black people in culture, there is a push toward associating Black people, young males especially, with criminality, deficiency, and inferiority. The author explains that these continued experiences of social defeat create disparities in Black people leading to higher levels of depression, mortality rates, unemployment, and psychological distress when compared to White people. This contributes to the Black individual being forced to assume the stance of the "defeated rat," avoiding social participation and being prevented from participating.

Delegitimization and Discrimination

Shepherd also cites Bar-Tal to describe delegitimization as a concept,

---

[97] Smith, A. (2012). Indigeneity, settler colonialism, white supremacy. *Racial formation in the twenty-first century, 66.*
[98] Shepherd, R. (2019). The Relationship Between the Repeated Social Defeat Stress Experimental Model, Delegitimization, and Neuroresilience in Experiences of Young African-American Males. *Journal of Underrepresented & Minority Progress, 3*(2), 99-108.

which is helpful here.[99] Delegitimization is a method of grouping individuals into social categories that denies any potential for their meaningful participation or inclusion in social activities. Doing so allows for moral exclusion. Common forms of delegitimization include dehumanization, negative trait characterization, outcasting, political labeling, and negative group comparison. It is intended to be a highly prejudicial and systematic process. In addition to associating strong negative cognitions concerning a delegitimized group, feelings such as anger, fear, and disgust are necessarily evoked, which then accompany implications that the group is a threat and, hence deserving sub-human treatment. This opens the pathway to harm.

Bar-Tal explains that an in-group that seeks to protect itself must position the out-group as being aggressive and capable of violence so that violence toward the out-group can then be legitimized. Violence from the in-group must occur in tandem with a sufficient amount of delegitimization. The endless cycle then is that violent mistreatment is a form of removing dignity, and removing dignity dehumanizes, which then permits more violence. The author cited the Holocaust and Nazi propaganda as contributing to the near-endless methods of dehumanizing Jews during World War II and the delegitimization of Black people as a justification for slavery and centuries-long practice of kidnapping, sexual assault, lynching, and violence.

What is key is that Bar-Tal explains the justification for delegitimization as the following:

- when the in-group sees the goals of the out-group as threatening the goals of the in-group;
- when the in-group sees the out-group as different and devalued, resulting in fear or contempt toward them; and
- when the in-group seeks to use extreme violence on the out-group.

Similar results are to be found all around the world. From the UK, Pearce and colleagues explain that, regardless of minority status, immigrants, ethnic minorities, visible minorities, and sexual minorities

---

[99] Bar-Tal, D. (1990). Causes and consequences of delegitimization: Models of conflict and ethnocentrism. *Journal of Social issues, 46*(1), 65-81.

experience higher rates of psychosis.[100] Their literature review explains that, with immigrants, it is not only the difficulty with coming to a new country because both first and second-generation incidence rates of psychosis occur along a similar average. In any case, they found that discrimination appears to be strongly linked to the emergence of psychosis and the exacerbation of psychiatric symptoms such as paranoia.

The authors explain that there is plenty of evidence to suggest that discrimination negatively impacts a person's physical, social, and mental health outcomes. Discrimination can be interpreted as being adverse experiences listed as social inequality, bullying, and other forms of mistreatment. Adverse experiences that relegate groups of individuals to being subordinate or outsiders impact the recipient's neurobiology, including their HPA axis functioning and other nervous system changes, which lead to further mental health vulnerabilities. Chronic experiences of discrimination give the common experiences of social threat, prevention of social participation, and humiliation.

As I have written elsewhere, perceived discrimination appears to take place more frequently among Black people than any other people.[101] Other researchers have also echoed this[102] but what is clear is that Black people are affected by stressors that do not appear to impact White people.

Adam and colleagues explain that what accounts for many of the health outcome disparities between racial groups could be based on perceived racial discrimination experiences.[103] Perceived racial discrimination is explained as having experienced or having perceived that

---

[100] Pearce, J., Rafiq, S., Simpson, J., & Varese, F. (2019). Perceived discrimination and psychosis: a systematic review of the literature. *Social Psychiatry and Psychiatric Epidemiology*, 1-22.
[101] Archer, D. (2020). Racial Trauma, Neurons, and EMDR: The Path Towards an Anti-Racist Psychotherapy. *Go With That Magazine.*
[102] Comas-Díaz, L., Hall, G. N., & Neville, H. A. (2019). Racial trauma: Theory, research, and healing: Introduction to the special issue. *American Psychologist*, 74(1), 1.
[103] Adam, E. K., Heissel, J. A., Zeiders, K. H., Richeson, J. A., Ross, E. C., Ehrlich, K. B., Levy, D.J., Kemeny, M.,
  Brodish, A.B., Malanchuk, O., & Peck, S. C. (2015). Developmental histories of perceived racial discrimination
  and diurnal cortisol profiles in adulthood: A 20-year prospective study. *Psychoneuroendocrinology, 62*, 279-291.

one has experienced racial discrimination due to their group membership—racial and ethnic minorities across the board report experiencing higher levels of discrimination than White people.

The White and Black Response to Police Violence

Bor and colleagues explain that it is not only a higher number of incidents of discrimination that a Black American will face but also that the nation is currently reckoning with a higher degree of police violence.[104] The authors explained that police officers kill black Americans at a rate of three times that of White Americans. What they found was that the impact of this form of state-sanctioned violence, as well as the repeated images and viewings on television, radio, social media, causes a mental health burden, resulting in distress and sick days that was almost as bad for Black Americans as the mental health burden of another health issue—diabetes.

But there still were differences, and here is where it gets interesting. When police officers killed unarmed Black men, as opposed to armed Black men, its effect on the Black community was substantially less than on White communities. Black Americans suffer a mental health spillover effect from seeing unarmed Black people killed in the media. Interestingly, White Americans did not see the same spillover effect for the killings of unarmed or armed White Americans. Not surprisingly, White Americans also did not need to take nearly as many sick days off work as Black Americans did when seeing their Black brethren killed by police. The authors found that White American participants were comparatively unaffected by the murder of Black Americans at the hands of police officers. White Americans were relatively unaffected by any police killing involving White or Black victims. In contrast, Black Americans were more greatly affected by police killings, regardless of the victim's race.

The authors explain that part of this disparity in the lack of mental health spillover effects for White people may be due to the long history of racial disparities in legal issues and law enforcement which are essential in systems of White supremacy. This makes it so that some groups will be

---

[104] Bor, J., Venkataramani, A. S., Williams, D. R., & Tsai, A. C. (2018). Police killings and their spillover effects on the mental health of black Americans: a population-based, quasi-experimental study. *The Lancet, 392*(10144), 302-310.

more affected than others. They explain that state-sanctioned violence has historically been used to terrorize and devalue the lives of Black Americans. They assert that police killings are a manifestation of systemic racism. They signal the implicit lower value of life placed on Black people in not only legal institutions but also by the general society.

Shame and Complex PTSD

Tobias and Joseph provide a description of the process of psychological abuse that takes place to legitimize police pressure on Black Canadians.[105] Carding is defined by the authors as an event where police officers approach an individual on the street without a warrant and request information about them. On a specific "card," the officer can record data for approximately 60 data points concerning any individual at their own discretion. The officer can then gather basic identifiable information about the citizen relating to age, gender, ethnicity, and race. This information then becomes permanently stored in police department databases. While the process is said to assist with policing, it highly depends on racial profiling. The authors consider this practice a form of macroaggression in that the practice is specifically directed at "Blackness" rather than a specific person. Here we call it macroaggression because it is also a common practice and a form of racial profiling that perpetuates racial practices within an institution and manages and preserves systemic racism.

Gaslighting is instrumental in maintaining any abusive relationship. Tobias and Joseph cite Roberts and Andrews,[106] explaining that it is a kind of psychological abuse that involves an abuser manipulating the physical and emotional state of the victim while simultaneously denying that the manipulation occurs and having the victim question whether the abuse actually transpired. This positions the abuser as authoritative and the victim as paranoid. With this dynamic, victims will come to second guess

---

[105] Tobias, H., & Joseph, A. (2020). Sustaining systemic racism through psychological gaslighting: Denials of racial profiling and justifications of carding by police utilizing local news media. *Race and Justice, 10*(4), 424-455.

[106] Roberts, T., & Andrews, D. C. (2013). *A critical race analysis of the gaslighting against African American teachers considerations for recruitment and retention.* In D. C. Andrews (Ed.), Contesting the myth of a "post racial" era: The continued significance of race in U.S. Education (Black Studies and Critical Thinking) (1st ed., pp. 69–94). New York, NY: Peter Lang.

their proper reality, relying instead on the abuser's judgment—which will predictably discount their own.

Selten and colleagues explain that what is contingent on social defeat is not just low income because there is no evidence of a higher-level risk of schizophrenia in low-income countries.[107] It is one's perception of having been defeated that increases the risk for the disorder. The authors explain that while social defeat may not cause schizophrenia, it is still a common denominator for several of its risk factors (e.g., urban upbringing, adverse childhood experiences, migration, illicit drug use, etc.).

Salter and Hall discuss the function of shame in our society. In this case, the authors situate shame as being an important part of the etiology and maintenance of complex Post Traumatic Stress Disorder (PTSD) symptoms.[108] Some aspects of shame and humiliation are systemic. The authors list examples that demonstrate that shame, which appears built into our societies, affects the general population at the levels of relationships, communities, institutions, and the macro-social level. Structural examples relate to neighborhood social disorganization as a product of social policy, historical patterns of genocide, dispossession, and discriminatory legislation. All of these impact one's sense of feeling defeated or excluded from the rest of the population. Those who are excluded members of a given population are more vulnerable to experiencing shame and humiliation.

Social Construction of Inequity

In terms of social exclusion, Brondolo and colleagues explain that racism interacts with non-race related stressors such as socioeconomic status and limited access to resources due to racially segregated neighborhoods.[109] The effects of social exclusion are consistent with one

---

[107] Selten, J. P., van der Ven, E., Rutten, B. P., & Cantor-Graae, E. (2013). The social defeat hypothesis of schizophrenia: an update. *Schizophrenia bulletin, 39(6)*, 1180-1186.

[108] Salter, M., & Hall, H. (2021) Reducing Shame, Promoting Dignity: A Model for the Primary Prevention of Complex Post-Traumatic Stress Disorder. *Trauma, Violence, & Abuse.*

[109] Brondolo, E., Ver Halen, N. B., Pencille, M., Beatty, D., & Contrada, R. J. (2009). Coping with racism: A selective review of the literature and a theoretical and methodological critique. *Journal of behavioral medicine, 32*(1), 64-88.

of the most detrimental effects of racism: structural racism.[110] Brondolo and colleagues consider structural racism as an important stressor for Black people. Historically, it was illegal for enslaved Black people to read. After emancipation, African Americans were still prevented from being included in intellectual pursuits by being forced to attend segregated and under-resourced schools. The authors continue by explaining that disproportionate poverty rates, housing discrimination, and residential segregation may stem from this historical past and that structural racism today severely limits opportunities for upward mobility for many Black people.

What I hope is clear now is that "race" and our perception of "Blackness" and its associative characteristics are socially constructed. However, within this socially constructed reality, society's views can and will impact an individual's self-concept, especially when these views are embedded in everyday language, used unconsciously, uncritically, and unopposed.[111] Also, as represented in media such as films and movies that depict racial minorities, popular culture often reflects and influences the societal views of a given racial group.[112] Black people may have a comparably different lived experience from Whites, especially because White people often do not connect their race to their everyday experience or their identity.[113]

What is important to understand is that the events which occurred in the past have set the groundwork for discrimination toward Black people in the present. Black suffering is not only what happened, but what is happening. The social construction of suffering must always be occurring at all times. This form of suffering may not cause mental illnesses, but it does open the possibility of vulnerabilities for them. What has been

---

[110] Kelly, S., Maynigo, P., Wesley, K., & Durham, J. (2013). African American communities and family systems: Relevance and challenges. *Couple and Family Psychology: Research and Practice*, 2(4), 264.

[111] Mohamed, C. & Smith, R. (1999). Race in the therapy relationship. In M. Lawrence, M. Maguire & J. Campling (Eds.), *Psychotherapy with women: feminist perspectives* (pp. 134-159). New York: Routledge.

[112] Childs, E. (2004). Interracial Images: Popular Culture Depictions of Black-White Couples. *Conference Papers—American Sociological Association*, 1-35.

[113] Todd, N. R., & Abrams, E. M. (2011). White dialectics: A new framework for theory, research, and practice with White students. *The Counseling Psychologist, 39,* 353-395.

discussed in this chapter will not only apply to Black people because all people exist within the racial spectrum of White and Black. Many of the other racial groups exist as "buffer classes" between the White/Black spectrum. There are chances that Brown people can treat Black people like this or that White people can treat Indigenous people in such a way. But it is key to understand that while the concept of in-groups and out-groups may be natural, the effects of racism are artificial, socially constructed, and intentionally maintained.

IN SUMMARY

Social defeat is a process initiated by the oppressor, which leads the oppressed to internalize the experience of being downtrodden. For it to be effective, it must be played out repetitively; the oppressed must always be portrayed as defeated. Whether the victim is rendered defeated or resistant, there is still a nervous system response that discourages further feelings of safety. It is necessary for the victim of Black suffering to believe they are deserving of violence through shame and inferiorization. But violence can only really take place if the offender disassociates the target from their humanity. This necessitates the need for constant delegitimization, which is grounded in competition, fear, and contempt. When questioned about the use of violence, gaslighting is necessary to cause the victim to question their sanity and maintain a pattern of violence.

A COMMENT ON BLACK SUFFERING

Despite being on the receiving end of all of this suffering, for White supremacy to continue, it is necessary that all Black people be able to "play it cool" as we are prone to do.[114] People who are delegitimized are not expected to protest in any shape or form. They are expected to remain defeated. The function of protest in any relationship implies that the status quo must be altered. It is likely that even this chapter can cause non-Black people to become uncomfortable. This may be, in part, because it focuses on some hypothesized mechanisms of Black suffering that are deeply embedded in the global collective psyche and renders what was unconscious to become conscious. There is always discomfort when the

---

[114] Grier, W. H., & Cobbs, P. M. (2000). *Black rage*. Wipf and Stock Publishers.

unconscious renders information to the level of perceived consciousness, especially when there is a socially encouraged active suppression of guilt or the maintenance of the appearance of a nation's "innocence." Relational dynamics only become alterable if we are aware that they exist. Your discomfort is acknowledged because no honest or compassionate person in their heart could ever be "cool" with this system. And once we all reach a critical mass, including White people, in recognizing that we no longer support these baseless racial hierarchies and that we no longer tacitly endorse social defeat by our institutions, then, and only then, will the status quo be pressured to change, once and forever.

BLACK SUFFERING

For White Supremacy to exist, a state of Black suffering must persist. Black people must always be in a state of constant and utter social defeat. It is an external and internal process.

THE CYCLE

Process of Inferiorization

Internalized Oppression

Maintenance of this cycle leads to a state of SHAME

SOCIAL DEFEAT

One rodent is in its territory, the other rodent is introduced

The territorial rodent must defend its territory

Repeated attacks and intimidation cause two responses: "defeat" or "resistance"†

DEFEAT
♦ Depressive/Anxious symptoms
♦ HPA axis sensitivity

 OR

RESISTANCE
♦ Anxious symptoms
♦ HPA axis activation

JUSTIFICATION FOR DELEGITIMIZATION**

- When the in-group sees the goals of the out-group as threatening
- When the in-group sees the out-group as different and devalued, leading to fear or contempt
- When the in-group seeks to use extreme violence on the out-group

VIOLENCE

- Violence cannot occur **without** delegitimization
- Violence is **also** a form of delegitimization
- The oppressed **must** be seen as socially defeated to encourage further delegitimization

*Dulka, B. N., Lynch III, J. F., Latsko, M. S., Mulvany, J. L., & Jasnow, A. M. (2015). Phenotypic responses to social defeat are associated with differences in cued and contextual fear discrimination. *Behavioural processes*, 118, 115-122.
**Bar-Tal, D. (1990). Causes and consequences of delegitimization: Models of conflict and ethnocentrism. *Journal of Social Issues*, 46(1), 65-81.

CHAPTER 7:

TRAUMA TRANSMISSION – YOUNG'S FIVE FACES OF OPPRESSION

Trauma History

She scanned the list with her eyes wide. Then she paused, smiled, and said, "This must be the longest trauma list you've ever seen."

"No, no," I replied. "Hate to break it to you, but it's not!"

"Dang it," she snapped her fingers, and we laughed.

The rapport was established. The alliance was formed. We had been working together for several sessions and got to the part where we listed the different traumatic events that affected her life. During this phase, we created our treatment plan.

The client's perspective changes once we can demonstrate that there are a finite number of traumatic events to be addressed. Therapy does not need to continue for an unlimited number of sessions. It can feel like we have been suffering for our whole lives, but there is generally a fixed number of "worst events" that we ever need to address in therapy.

This can make therapy more manageable; it allows us to see the light at the end of the tunnel. There is both a sense of excitement and relief when we can list the origins of our suffering. It allows us to see that we ourselves are not "bad," but that we have all just survived "bad" things.

It is important for us to be conscious of our treatment plan. Recording the trauma history allows us to see our patterns. Once we are conscious of our unconscious patterns, then we get the chance to change our future.

It is necessary not only to consider the past but all of the stressors that may be impacting the client in the present. In this chapter, we will consider the role of oppression and its various manifestations as they impact not only our societies but also the institutions that we are a part of.

The Complex Interplay of White Supremacy and Black Suffering

It is my belief then that the "trauma" of White supremacy and Black suffering is "complex." While PTSD is commonly associated with thought intrusions, avoidance of traumatic reminders, a negative mood, and a state of hypervigilance,[115] Salter and Hall explain that Complex Post Traumatic Stress Disorder (CPTSD) is an advanced form of the previous disorder.[116] Thought to occur due to exposure to early childhood trauma, and prolonged and chronic interpersonal abuse, the authors cite Herman,[117] explaining that CPTSD additionally has symptoms which resemble dissociative identity disorder, borderline personality disorder (BPD), and other mental and emotional disturbances. Similar to Brüne, the authors explain that some of the symptoms of CPTSD may be a result of maladaptive coping mechanisms from an unpredictable early environment. Though Brüne describes the behavioral manifestations and schemas of the borderline personality patient, the explanation still holds: it is explained that "children who are exposed to environmental cues such

---

[115] American Psychiatric Association. (2013). *Diagnostic and statistical manual of mental disorders: DSM-5.* Washington, D.C: American Psychiatric Association.
[116] Salter, M., & Hall, H. (2021). Reducing Shame, Promoting Dignity: A Model for the Primary Prevention of Complex Post-Traumatic Stress Disorder. *Trauma, Violence, & Abuse.*
[117] Herman, J. (1992). *Trauma and Recovery.* New York: Basic Books.

as harsh parenting, violence or other sources of danger are more likely to develop an inner working model suggesting that the availability of future resources is scarce." [118] Hence, because of one's past life history, they develop a present strategy for operating in the world.

Note:

Because CPTSD is often not discussed and is poorly understood, I must take a moment to list some of its essential traits as it does not always present in severe forms. CPTSD comprises the main symptoms of PTSD but also "includes symptoms of disturbances in self-organization (DSO; affect dysregulation, negative self-concept, and disturbances in relationships)." [119] The effects of these impairments have previously been cited in the literature as "disorders of extreme stress not otherwise specified" (DESNOS). DESNOS involves:

persistent alterations in seven aspects of self-regulation and psychosocial functioning following exposure to traumatic stress: (a) affect and impulse regulation (i.e., persistent distress, risky behavior or self-harm), (b) biological self-regulation (i.e., somatization—pain or physical symptoms or impairments that cannot be fully medically explained), (c) attention or consciousness (i.e., dissociation), (d) perception of perpetrator or perpetrators (e.g., idealization, preoccupation with revenge), (e) self-perception (e.g., self as damaged or ineffective, profound shame or guilt), (f) relationships (e.g., inability to trust, revictimization, avoidance of sexuality), and

---

[118] Brüne, M. (2016). Borderline Personality Disorder Why 'fast and furious'?. *Evolution, medicine,*
and public health, 2016(1), 52-66.
[119] Knefel, M., Lueger-Schuster, B., Karatzias, T., Shevlin, M., & Hyland, P. (2019).
From child maltreatment to ICD-11 complex post-traumatic stress symptoms: The role of emotion regulation and re-victimisation. *Journal of clinical psychology, 75*(3), 392-393.

> (g) systems of meaning or sustaining beliefs (e.g., hopelessness, loss of faith).[120]

When the liberal White person claims "color blindness" or not "seeing color" when speaking to a Black or Brown person, it can be interpreted as a form of dissociation. Distancing oneself from one's experience allows for the nullification of any grief or guilt concerning the concept of White supremacy. This permits White supremacy to avoid confrontation and continue in operation. When the Black person is continuously exposed to videos of Black people being harmed by police officers on social media and then later is in a state of hypervigilance upon seeing a police officer in his rearview mirror, we see that Black suffering is maintained and brought into reality. Addressing the racial injustice incites the gaslighting. The White person does not see race. The Black person is, in fact, defeated and always will be. The final defeat occurs once the Black person internalizes it. White supremacy wins. Again. Again. And Again.

Shengold describes a process of "soul murder," which relates to our concept of social defeat.[121] When talking about the effects of extreme and chronic child abuse, soul murder occurs when there are deliberate attempts to completely destroy the identity of another individual with less power, leaving them in complete bondage and dependence on another. This is one way of seeing the extent of racism and colonialism. Schwartz also discusses this process of internalized oppression, which complex trauma survivors experience through victimhood. The explanation is that the goal of the sadistic abuser is to transform the "innocent" victim into themselves. Schwartz writes, "When innocents can be trained to 'choose' to repeatedly betray themselves and betray other innocents without overt signals from the perpetrator(s), the hand of evil is off the wheel and the machinery of destructiveness becomes self-perpetuating and self-sustaining. *Such a*

---

[120] Ford, J. D., Stockton, P., Kaltman, S., & Green, B. L. (2006). Disorders of extreme stress (DESNOS) symptoms are associated with type and severity of interpersonal trauma exposure in a sample of healthy young women. *Journal of Interpersonal Violence*, *21*(11), 1399-1416.

[121] Shengold, L. (1991). *Soul murder: The effects of childhood abuse and deprivation.* BoD–Books on Demand.

malignant arrangement exponentiates 'duping delight' (Salter, 1995) and maniacally inflates the omnipotence of diabolical perpetrators who may then experience uncontrollable fantasies of limitless power." [122]

The interplay of White supremacy and Black suffering and their resulting effects are designed to be like unwanted gifts that keep on giving. They are self-perpetuating and endless packages delivered without permission. Still, I would like to explain how the processes of suffering are transmitted, maintained, and replicated through institutions and social arrangements. There are specific means of transmission that are necessary to make conscious so that we can identify them, recognize them, and respond accordingly.

Categorizing Oppression Inside and Outside of the Office

What I would like to use first is Young's model of the Five Faces of Oppression.[123] Young views oppression as systemic in nature and that, for each group that is oppressed, there is an opposing group that experiences an advantage because of this. It's a balancing act. On some level, the cost to one oppressed group leads to a benefit experienced by another. When crafting an anti-racist practice, we have to ask ourselves, do we do any of this? You can ask yourself as we follow along.

Young's Five Faces of Oppression:

- Cultural Imperialism
- Exploitation
- Powerlessness
- Marginalization
- Violence

Cultural Imperialism

I would like to start with cultural imperialism because I see it as the

---

[122] Schwartz, H. L. (2013). *The alchemy of wolves and sheep: A relational approach to internalized perpetration in complex trauma survivors*. Routledge.

[123] Young, I. M. (2000). Five faces of oppression. In M. Adams, W. J. Blumenfeld, R. Castaneda, H. W. Hackman, M. L. Peters, & X. Zuniga (Eds.), *Readings for diversity and social justice: An anthology on racism, antisemitism, sexism, heterosexism, ableism and classism* (pp. 35-49). New York: Routledge.

most powerful and relevant. Cultural imperialism is explained as a means of universalizing the experience of White people, centering them as the norm and the standard. When watching Hollywood movies directed mostly by White men, we see a White hetero-normative perspective on the world, consume it, and internalize it as normal. We largely see the world through a Eurocentric perspective and are taught to do so by our institutions.[124] Cultural imperialism then occurs when we universalize the experience and culture of Whiteness.

Gilbert explains that the field of counseling is offered and experienced by people whose backgrounds do not resemble those who originally developed it.[125] Most psychotherapies rely on a Western conception of the "self." Our understanding of self could actually be more complex or diverse than how Western cultures see it. In some cultures, the self exists in conjunction with other family members or social structures. Our Western psychotherapy models are thus insufficient in those contexts and can only be applied with appropriate modification.

Hinton and Simon's chapter on cultural neuroscience suggests that there is not one uniform way that people experience anxiety disorders.[126] Although Cambodian and Vietnamese refugees have high rates of PTSD, triggers that cause a panic attack can range from being hit by a cold wind or standing up from a sitting position. These are survivors of trauma; the negative cognitions related to their triggers are based on cultural histories as survivors of genocide and state-sanctioned violence. Without sufficient cultural awareness, we can miss this or, worse still, deny that it is relevant.

Question: Are we teaching professionals from a strictly Eurocentric perspective? Are we teaching trauma therapists to recognize differences?

---

[124] Williams, M. T. (2019). Adverse racial climates in academia: Conceptualization, interventions,
and call to action. *New ideas in Psychology*, *55*, 58-67.
[125] Gilbert, J. (2006). Cultural imperialism revisited: Counselling and globalisation. *International Journal of Critical Psychology*, *17*, 10-28.
[126] Hinton, D. E., & Simon, N. (2015). Toward a Cultural Neuroscience of Anxiety Disorders: The Multiplex Model. In L. Kirmayer, R. Lemelson, & C. Cummings (Eds.), *Re-Visioning Psychiatry: Cultural Phenomenology, Critical Neuroscience, and Global Mental Health* (pp. 343-374). Cambridge: Cambridge University Press. doi:10.1017/CBO9781139424745.017

Exploitation

Young explains that the right to claim the product of others' labor defines the privilege of class. Exploitation refers to the ability to dominate another group and benefit from their work. The use of the oppressed person's labor and energy improves the wealth and well-being of the dominating group. In a way, you are working hard for someone and set up to depend on them, so you are forced to continue. Slavery is the most obvious example of this. If we are talking about contemporary examples, you will see that, in most situations, those who do manual labor are often Black or Brown people. If you have ever been on a cruise or a resort, you will see who works hard and who benefits.

For the mental health and helping fields, unpaid internships have often been a hotly contested issue. In part because, despite the important work of the students in training, they are not always fairly compensated, if at all. The moral and ethical questions that arise considering this are many, especially since this phenomenon is especially apparent in female-dominated fields.[127][128]

Question: Does exploitation happen in our training and regular business practices? Has this been normalized in our fields of practice?

Powerlessness

Powerlessness refers to those who have influence and those who do not. This form of oppression is fairly common when you know where to look. Because work relationships are not democratic, they often function from a hierarchical perspective; the employee follows the will of the employer. Titles confer power. Young explains that there is a privilege that separates those who are seen as professionals and those who are not. The powerless are explained as those who lack authority and, in certain cases, power is exerted over them without the oppressor needing to take action.

---

[127] Shade, L. R., & Jacobson, J. (2015). Hungry for the job: gender, unpaid internships, and the
creative industries. *The Sociological Review, 63*(S1), 188-205.
[128] McHugh, P. P. (2017). The impact of compensation, supervision and work design on internship efficacy: implications for educators, employers and prospective interns. *Journal of Education and Work, 30*(4), 367-382.

Powerlessness is the inability to alter our destiny—the inability to have autonomy or carry through with decisions.

The dynamic of powerlessness is frequently seen in situations relating to gender or sexual harassment. Herbenick and colleagues explain that sexual harassment can, in some cases, be exacerbated by being in a lower position of power.[129] This means that those whom are students, people of color, sexual minorities, and other marginalized demographics are at greater risk of being victimized, even in academic settings.

Capawana explains, similarly, that power also impacts our practice.[130] In his literature review, he explains that sexually intimate behavior between psychologists, supervisees, clients, and students is a serious problem. The author cites additional researchers, explaining that men who work in the mental health field are more likely to be perpetrators of sexual misconduct. Still, although those most often seen as sexual aggressors are overrepresented as males, and though female therapists are less likely to be perpetrators, both genders are more likely to enact sexual boundary violations with female clients. Hence power still disproportionately affects women, necessitating the need for considerations of feminist practice regardless of one's socially constructed gender identity.

Question: Are we sufficiently training therapists to not abuse their power? What protections or means are there of mitigating these issues?

Marginalization

Young considers this form of oppression as the most dangerous. You can cause a whole group or category of people from having any meaningful participation in a social structure. Social exclusion is a form of this, the fact that you may not have heard from any other Black male psychotherapists before is another. The paradox of being marginalized is that you are both important and unimportant. You are relegated to the sides

---

[129] Herbenick, D., van Anders, S. M., Brotto, L. A., Chivers, M. L., Jawed-Wessel, S., & Galarza, J.
(2019). Sexual harassment in the field of sexuality research. *Archives of sexual behavior*, 48(4), 997-1006.
[130] Capawana, M. (2016). Intimate attractions and sexual misconduct in the therapeutic relationship: Implications for socially just practice. *Cogent Psychology, 3*(1), 1-13.

but given a label or an acronym. Black people exist as the topic of conversation but rarely as the director; we are the pathology but not the professional who assesses it.

Williams explains that marginalization occurs quite often in academia.[131] In the United States Census reports, 13% of the population is Black, and 18% are Hispanic, yet, in higher education faculty, 6% are Black, and 5% are Hispanic. Hispanic and Black professors in the United States are underrepresented, and when they do become professors, they are rarely full professors or higher-level administrators; instead, they occupy assistant or adjunct professor roles.

Question: Are there sufficient numbers of psychologists, counselors, social workers, psychotherapists, and other mental health interveners who are also BIPOC? LGBTQ? Do we see these people reflected in our media?

Violence

With this specific face of oppression, Young explains that it is not just the act of violence that makes it oppressive, but it is the context in which it occurs. Violence occurs in places and in ways for specific groups in which it will not for other groups. Williams also explains that racial microaggressions occur at a higher rate for both faculty and students of color in higher education. Experiences of discrimination occur at a higher level for Black people who have higher levels of education in part because they may need to navigate being in spaces where they live and work in contexts where they are not expected to be, namely predominantly White spaces.[132]

Young explains that violence becomes a social injustice when it becomes so frequent and so unchallenged that it becomes a matter of social

---

[131] Williams, M. T. (2019). Adverse racial climates in academia: Conceptualization, interventions,
and call to action. *New ideas in Psychology, 55*, 58-67.
[132] Adam, E. K., Heissel, J. A., Zeiders, K. H., Richeson, J. A., Ross, E. C., Ehrlich, K. B., Levy, D.J., Kemeny, M.,
Brodish, A.B., Malanchuk, O., & Peck, S. C. (2015). Developmental histories of perceived racial discrimination
and diurnal cortisol profiles in adulthood: A 20-year prospective study. *Psychoneuroendocrinology, 62*, 279-291.

practice.

The Washington Post attempted to log every police shooting in the United States by on-duty police officers.[133] They found it interesting that despite the lack of predictability that precedes a police shooting, the number of people shot and killed has been relatively stable each year since 2015. There are approximately 1000 people shot and killed in the United States each year. They explain that Black Americans are killed by police officers more than twice as often as White Americans and that most of those shot are young men.

Question: Because there has not been any such widespread condemnation of the act until 2020, and also because, at the time of writing this, many of the police officers who have killed Black people are often not charged, does this confer as being a social injustice or even a social practice?

Aside from physical violence, it is necessary to discuss a lesser-known manifestation of violence, which is considered here as a category of violence: microaggressions.

Microaggressions are defined as commonplace; every day, verbal, non-verbal, or environmental instances of disrespect[134] can take the form of racist jokes, Facebook memes, and ambiguous slights. Facebook memes are included in that many users will frequently use animated gifs that show Black people's expressions and may be used extensively by White people to perform what is called digital blackface.[135] Touching one's hair without consent or making obscure comments that are meant to degrade the individual in a subtle way are violent by design.

Williams and colleagues found that these violent actions do not need

---

[133] The Washington Post. (2020) *Fatal Force [Database that records police shootings in the United States].* Retrieved December 14, 2020 from
https://www.washingtonpost.com/graphics/investigations/police-shootings-database/
[134] Sue, D. W., Capodilupo, C. M., Torino, G. C., Bucceri, J. M., Holder, A., Nadal, K. L., & Esquilin, M. (2007). Racial microaggressions in everyday life: implications for clinical practice. *American psychologist, 62*(4), 271
[135] Jones, E. E. (2018, July 8). Why are memes of black people reacting so popular online?. *The Guardian.* https://www.theguardian.com/culture/2018/jul/08/why-are-memes-of-black-people-reacting-so-popular-online

to be only verbal; these can include how we are portrayed or how we are excluded.[136] The authors found that BIPOC individuals experienced these events much more frequently than White participants. Additionally, the more that BIPOC participants experienced them in their real everyday life, the more susceptible they were to observe them online. Once more, this is a form of violence that can often go undetected by White people, although White people can commit it.

The Connection to Trauma

It is important to understand that while there are innumerable categories for how adverse experiences affect others, the Five Faces of Oppression are a way of categorizing them. Cultural imperialism is encountered by people of color when they are experienced at being an 'other' or misled to believe that their way of being is wrong or unjust. Exploitation can occur in terms of our interpersonal relationships with others on an emotional, mental, spiritual, or physical level. Powerlessness transpires when people of color are denied their voice or their free will. Marginalization is when those with different complexions or hair types are excluded from categories where one would find dignity and respect. And violence, as stated above, does not need to be physical. Emotional and verbal forms can, in some cases, be even worse because the human eye does not perceive the scars.

While big-T traumas like war or famine are often discussed on the news, the small-t traumas of glass ceilings and microaggressions are rarely discussed. This does not preclude them from being traumatic. Any individual who works in the field of mental health must consider that oppression exists on a spectrum, and though we may disagree on what constitutes violence for the client, their nervous system will beg to differ.

IN SUMMARY

What is important to understand is the role that oppression plays in our daily activities. There is something about our society that tends to allow or legitimize certain forms of violence toward certain people. In this

---

[136] Williams, A., Oliver, C., Aumer, K., & Meyers, C. (2016). Racial microaggressions and perceptions of Internet memes. *Computers in Human Behavior, 63*, 424-432.

way, we are all survivors and/or descendants of survivors of trauma. We learn to adapt either by avoiding the trauma, healing the trauma, or victimizing ourselves or others. The form of transmission of trauma is not limited by Young's Five Faces of Oppression, but each can be used as menacing tactics that invoke soul murder, consolidated once and for all, especially when the victim sees themselves as deserving of it. Thus, it is necessary for us to assist others in naming the problem so that they do not see themselves as the problem. It is the first step but necessary step in restoring the inherent dignity that all souls on this planet are entitled to see as their natural birthright.

TRAUMA TRANSMISSION AND YOUNG'S FIVE FACES OF OPPRESSION

Adverse experiences can either be traumatic or non-traumatic. Either way, they can lead to to the creation of pathogenic memories.

RACE IS ORGANIZED AROUND TRAUMA

Soul Murder

WHITE SUPREMACY	BLACK SUFFERING
Dissociates from Trauma	Associated with Trauma

└── Validates ──┘

PTSD   COMPLEX PTSD

CAN BE THE RESULT OF

A single event

Multiple Events
Early Childhood
Trauma Chronic
Interpersonal Abuse

YOUNG'S FIVE FACES OF OPPRESSION*

Explains how categories of actions, policies, and beliefs can lead to the oppression of specific groups.

Cultural Imperialism
Universalization of one culture's experience

Exploitation
Use of the oppressed labor and energy to unfairly benefit

Powerlessness
Removal of influence, denial of agency

Violence
Covert and overt forms of aggression

Marginalization
Exclusion from meaningful social participation

*Young, I. M. (2000). Five faces of oppression. In M. Adams, W. J. Blumenfeld, R. Castaneda, H. W. Hackman, M. L. Peters, & X. Zuniga (Eds.), *Readings for diversity and social justice: An anthology on racism, antisemitism, sexism, heterosexism, ableism and classism* (pp. 35-49). New York: Routledge.

PART THREE:
NEUROSCIENCE, STRESS, AND
PSYCHOTHERAPY

CHAPTER 8:

INTERNALIZED OPPRESSION AND

HOMEOSTASIS

Self-Hatred

"I fucking hate them!" the client exclaimed. I jumped back, startled. I was a novice therapist and was unaware of the fact that my gesture to listen would be met with such a strong response.

"Hate? Hate who?" I nervously sputtered.

"White people!" the client cried.

Her tears streamed down her face, falling onto her scarred forearms. The client's scars carried memories of razor blades, formed during fits of adolescent rage and angst. While discussing the mistreatment done by the client's caregivers, there was no more damage that could be done other than to curse her oppressors.

In this case, though, the client was biracial. Being both Black and White, hating one of your parents inevitably leads to resenting the other. For then, how else could either parent make the error of your creation? The paradox of internalized oppression leads us to resent society's capacity for mistreatment while simultaneously cursing ourselves. We end up becoming upset with both the victim and the oppressor. The client grew to hate the privilege and the disadvantage.

This hostile world itself ceased to be welcoming.

In addition to the traumatic events themselves, the way how they are registered in our minds and the effects they carry on our nervous systems must be considered. This chapter will take a deep dive into the neurobiology of trauma and how it links to racial trauma.

The Effects of Internalized Oppression

Virginia Satir played a large influence in our understanding of relational systems. She was a family therapist who knew the importance of being "fully human." She explained in her book that while there are many different personality types, the importance and maintenance of self-esteem was paramount in all of them. Self-esteem cannot be preserved in the context of comparison.[137] If we say that one individual is worth more than another, then we are to create a value judgment. Someone always loses out when we make a comparison between them and normalcy. These losses of self-esteem, and our belief in subordination, render us less "human," which feeds into the process of delegitimization.

Salter and Hall cite Herman[138] when discussing the primacy of shame as it relates to complex trauma. The authors explain that there are higher levels of mental illness among marginalized groups, trauma exposure is unevenly distributed among different groups (especially regarding race, gender, and socioeconomic status), and there is an intergenerational component to the etiology of CPTSD.[139]

The authors mention that shame is important for the maintenance and

---

[137] Satir, V. (1988). *The New Peoplemaking*. New York. Science and Behavior Books, Inc.

[138] Herman, J. (1992). *Trauma and Recovery*. New York: Basic Books.

[139] Salter, M., & Hall, H. (2020). Reducing shame, promoting dignity: a model for the primary prevention of complex post-traumatic stress disorder. *Trauma, Violence, & Abuse*, 1524838020979667.

etiology of complex trauma. Additionally, in Dr. Hall's co-presentation on "Human Evil and Societal Trauma" at the International Society for the Study of Trauma and Dissociation (ISSTD) conference in 2020, a discussion of psychopathy, narcissistic personality, and child exploitation took place. In this presentation, Hall explained that shame is perhaps a motivator for the narcissistic personality type's victimization of others. It is especially important for the narcissistic abuser to have the victim admit that they are deserving of the abuse before they relent on the violence. It seems like shame, too, is part of this dichotomy between Blackness and Whiteness in a similar way. The retraumatization of racial trauma is intentionally repetitive, chronic, and shameful. I believe that the constant reminders of social defeat for Blackness are meant to assuage the perpetrator's fear of worthlessness, the shame relating to the myth of White supremacy.

The whole personhood of the White person can be threatened by the Black person, not by the Black person's action, but by the characteristics of their being. These comparative analyses unconsciously commit an assault on the self-esteem of White consciousness. The reaction to maintain balance and restore self-esteem is to assert White dominance and Black inferiority. It is for this reason that Black people are pressured to wear White masks.[140]

The effect of White supremacy on the Black individual is not just a singular event. What adds insult to injury is when the Black person experiences the echoes of pain and suffering throughout the generations. I speak here of what Dr. Joy DeGruy terms as Post Traumatic Slave Syndrome, which is:

> "a condition that exists when a population has experienced multigenerational trauma resulting from centuries of slavery and continues to experience oppression and institutionalized racism today.

---

[140] Fanon, F. (1970). *Black skin, white masks* (pp. 13-30). London: Paladin.

Added to this is a belief (real or imagined) that the benefits of the society in which they live are not accessible to them."[141]

In her important work, she goes on to speak about the impact that these beliefs have on the Black individual, their relation to others, and their participation in their own community.

The myth of Black inferiority becomes especially powerful as we internalize it into our minds and actions and its impact on our nervous system. The use of shame and the constant attacks on self-esteem have devastating effects on one's emotional well-being and the nervous system of those affected by the damaging effects of racial trauma.

Racial Trauma

Comas Diaz, Hall, and Neville introduce their article explaining that racism is responsible for ethnic and racial health disparities, that racial microaggressions affect physical and mental health, and that African Americans are exposed to racial discrimination more than any other group.

The authors define it as such: "Racial trauma, or race-based stress, refers to the events of danger related to real or perceived experience of racial discrimination."[142]

The authors explain that this type of trauma is unique in that it attacks not only the individual and their sense of self but also the community they are a part of. The trauma that Native Americans experienced, that Japanese Americans experienced, and what Latino communities are experiencing south of the border these events that occurred in the past through generations are echoed in the present. It is for these reasons I explain that racial trauma is a complex form of trauma; it is not just post-traumatic. It

---

[141] DeGruy, J. (2005). *Post Traumatic Slave Syndrome* (p. 105). Portland: Joy De Gruy Publications Inc.

[142] Comas-Díaz, L., Hall, G. N., & Neville, H. A. (2019). Racial trauma: Theory, research, and healing: Introduction to the special issue. *American Psychologist*, *74*(1), 1.

is also reinforced in the present at the interpersonal and nervous system level.[143]

> **Note:**
>
> While racial trauma is not, as of this time of writing, a clinical diagnosis, the effects of racial trauma are similar to post-traumatic stress disorder (PTSD). Although it is not considered as a clinical diagnosis in its own right, Williams suggests that racial trauma can merit a DSM-5 diagnosis of PTSD in certain conditions, as well as when certain ICD-10 criteria are taken into account[144]. However, as will be explained, racial trauma can, in some ways, be more complex than a PTSD diagnosis on its own.

Neurological Effects of Chronic Stress

From a neurological point of view, PTSD is essentially a loss of top-down inhibition over the limbic area (e.g., amygdala). There is an emotional over and under modulation that occurs with people who have PTSD. They explain that both PTSD and CPTSD, which occur with dissociative traits, are characterized as an inability or impairment of the cortical midline structures to manage the limbic areas. This leads to a hyperactivation of the amygdala (responsible for threat detection) and a hypoactivation of the medial prefrontal cortex (designed to make sense of the threat).[145] This is the reason why, with PTSD, we see the proverbial traumatized soldier who dives under a desk after hearing a loud bang in the office. The soldier has difficulty recontextualizing to his environment. It is not the actual content but the perception of the content that causes stress to the soldier.

---

[143] Archer, D. (2020). Racial Trauma, Neurons, and EMDR: The Path Towards an Anti-Racist Psychotherapy. *Go With That Magazine.*

[144] Williams, M. T. (2019, February 13). Uncovering the Trauma of Racism. *American Psychological Association.* https://www.apa.org/pubs/highlights/spotlight/issue-128

[145] Boyd, J. E., Lanius, R. A., & McKinnon, M. C. (2018). Mindfulness-based treatments for posttraumatic stress disorder: a review of the treatment literature and neurobiological evidence. *Journal of psychiatry & neuroscience: JPN, 43*(1), 7.

While there is much discussion about stress, it may be necessary before continuing to address what stress may actually be. The following is summarized by Adam and colleagues.[146] The hypothalamic-pituitary-adrenal axis (HPA axis) is an important biological system responsible for responding to stress or challenges to the safety and security of a human being. One of the important products of the HPA axis is the glucocorticoid hormone cortisol. Cortisol is important for the following reasons:

- It responds to both social and psychological stressors, whether they are acute or chronic.
- Early adverse experiences can impact the development and operation in later adult life.
- Cortisol has significant impacts on the entire organism, body and brain included.
- Cortisol also appears to be involved in a wide range of both physical and mental health conditions.

It is important to note that the HPA axis is designed to respond to stress or habituate to it, but some issues can affect its regular functioning.

The Multigenerational Transmission of Trauma

O'Brien explains that the study of epigenetics relates to how events that occur in one's environment can lead to changes in one's genetic sequence.[147] Not only is it that severely stressful events can leave an imprint on one's genes, but some genetic changes from a stressor can be inherited in later generations.

For a moment, it will be necessary to discuss the aspects which relate to the multigenerational transmission of trauma. Note that, in these cases,

---

[146] Adam, E. K., Quinn, M. E., Tavernier, R., McQuillan, M. T., Dahlke, K. A., & Gilbert, K. E. (2017). Diurnal cortisol slopes and mental and physical health outcomes: A systematic review and meta-analysis. *Psychoneuroendocrinology, 83,* 25-41.
[147] O'Brien, K. J. (2007) *The Uncounted Casualties of War: Epigenetics and the Intergenerational Transference of PTSD Symptoms among Children and Grandchildren of Vietnam Veterans in Australia.* https://eprints.qut.edu.au/13794/1/13794.pdf, accessed November 11, 2020.

these are actual large scale, "capital letter T trauma" events that seem to leave a genetic mark on individuals and their offspring.

While there are many studies, I will highlight some that specifically highlight essential points. Yehuda and colleagues conducted a study relating to the effects on pregnant women and those who witnessed the 2001 World Trade Center attacks.[148] They demonstrated that there are lower cortisol levels in mothers who developed PTSD after witnessing the terrorist attack than those who did not. We discuss mothers here because the offspring of these mothers also exhibited lower cortisol levels suggesting that there may have been a transmission of this trait during the gestational period. The authors suggest that increases in glucocorticoids caused by stress during pregnancy not only influence the development of the child in utero but influence the youth's brain development, which can cause permanent changes in the child's development.

Perroud and colleagues released a landmark study talking about the hypothalamic-pituitary-adrenal axis (HPA axis) in 2014.[149] This involved studying the effects of exposure to the Rwandan genocide of 1994 for survivors who had PTSD symptoms and the subsequent transmission of biological alterations to their offspring. They found that parental PTSD appeared to lead to an increased risk for the subsequent generation to be vulnerable to their mental health challenges; that these traumatized mothers may have also transmitted alterations to the HPA axis which would be inherited by their young; and that there were specific gene alterations in both the mother exposed to the armed conflict and the unborn child, meaning that the effects of trauma exposure could be very long-lasting.

Another significant study by Yehuda and colleagues related to the multigenerational trauma transmission of Jewish survivors of the

---

[148] Yehuda, R., Engel, S. M., Brand, S. R., Seckl, J., Marcus, S. M., & Berkowitz, G. S. (2005). Transgenerational effects of posttraumatic stress disorder in babies of mothers exposed to the World Trade Center attacks during pregnancy. *The Journal of Clinical Endocrinology & Metabolism, 90*(7), 4115-4118.

[149] Perroud, N., Rutembesa, E., Paoloni-Giacobino, A., Mutabaruka, J., Mutesa, L., Stenz, L., & Karege, F. (2014). The Tutsi genocide and transgenerational transmission of maternal stress: epigenetics and biology of the HPA axis. *The World Journal of Biological Psychiatry, 15*(4), 334-345.

Holocaust.[150] The researchers were interested in the genetic changes resulting from exposure to this large scale event. What they found was similar to the other studies but in this case, even exposure to preconception stress for both parents was enough to trigger an intergenerational priming effect leading to an increased risk of psychopathology in the following generation.

O'Brien reported similar experiences with veterans who conceived after being exposed to the atrocities of the Vietnam War. Children and grandchildren of Vietnam War veterans appeared to demonstrate PTSD symptoms, although they themselves did not experience any severe traumatic event. The information, which may have been adaptive for the traumatized individual to avoid a specific danger or to have a fixation on certain objects or words, can be passed onto the child where it is no longer adaptive or useful. The evolutionary inheritance of urges, behaviors, and predispositions that would ensure survival may have granted us an advantage in our prehistoric past, but the activation of these genes from stresses in our current environment can activate genes that increase our vulnerability to mental health disorders. The study of epigenetics helps to inform our understanding of the multigenerational transmission of stress vulnerabilities. But epigenetics may also explain why the prevalence of the PTSD diagnosis may increase over time.[151]

It is important to note then that when discussing responses to stress, we cannot just look at the moment when the proverbial straw breaks the camel's back. We must consider the build-up and accumulation of repeated stresses and the condition that the stress response system is already in before making a judgment of it.

---

[150] Yehuda, R., Daskalakis, N. P., Bierer, L. M., Bader, H. N., Klengel, T., Holsboer, F., & Binder, E. B. (2016). Holocaust exposure induced intergenerational effects on FKBP5 methylation. *Biological psychiatry*, *80*(5), 372-380.

[151] O'Brien, K. J. (2007) *The Uncounted Casualties of War: Epigenetics and the Intergenerational Transference of PTSD Symptoms among Children and Grandchildren of Vietnam Veterans in Australia.* https://eprints.qut.edu.au/13794/1/13794.pdf, accessed November 11, 2020.

Allostatic Load and Chronic Stress

While we have previously discussed homeostasis, it is imperative to discuss allostatic load. Juster, McEwen, and Lupien explain allostatic load as the "wear and tear" that the organism experiences in response to multiple stresses.[152] It is essential to understand that stresses can be either real or perceived, and the body will not distinguish between the two of them. Stresses invoke the fight/flight responses in an evolutionary adaptive way. But while these responses are adaptive for survival in acute conditions, when they are employed chronically and over-activated, the HPA axis and other biological systems then produce a cascade or domino effect of a failure of other biological systems, which reduces the body's capacity to protect itself against disease and reduce the capacity to reliably respond to future stressors.

McEwen explains that while the body itself seeks homeostasis, it can only do so by allostasis.[153] Allostasis relates to how different biological systems (cardiovascular, metabolic, immune, and central nervous system) shift operations and functions throughout the day and in response to the needs of the internal and external circumstances. Allostasis is related to when an individual is coping with a perceived challenge. States such as anxiousness and the excitatory state of anticipation places demands on the allostatic load, but when these states are maintained for too long, this leads to allostatic overload.

Simply put, chronic stresses lead to over activation of the HPA axis, and the prolonged secretion of stress hormones, instead of being adaptive, ends up damaging the body and nervous system.

As the body continues in this state, our biological systems compensate and alter their normal operating capacities. These alterations in normal operating capacities then cause allostatic overload, which results in disease, disorder, and dysfunction.

---

[152] Juster, R. P., McEwen, B. S., & Lupien, S. J. (2010). Allostatic load biomarkers of chronic stress and impact on health and cognition. *Neuroscience & Biobehavioral Reviews, 35*(1), 2-16.

[153] McEwen, B. S. (2006). Protective and damaging effects of stress mediators: central role of the brain. *Dialogues in clinical neuroscience, 8*(4), 367.

Allostatic overload worsens one's physical health due to these sustained hits to the system; prolonged and chronic stress is placed on our nervous system, metabolism, cardiovascular, and immune functions.

The Effects of Discrimination on Our Nervous System

McEwen continues further, explaining that the effects of chronic stress lead to physical changes in our brain's physical structure. The hippocampus, for example, is related to the limbic system and is implicated in long term memory. Any impairment to the hippocampus leads to inaccurate appraisals of the reliability and accuracy of memories as well as our future perception of stressful events. In a way, chronic stress distorts how some memories are stored, so this impacts our judgment about the future, which would then rely on faulty predictions. It is important to note that the hippocampus plays a role in regulating the HPA axis. During moments of acute stress, the effects on the brain are reversible, but when the stresses are chronic, repetitive, and prolonged for months or years, dendrites can begin to atrophy. The neurons of the hippocampus can die off.

McEwen describes the process as structural remodeling, in that chronic stress can atrophy neurons in the prefrontal cortex (designed for regulatory processes), in the hippocampus (relating to memory), but can hypertrophy or increase the density of the amygdala (responsible for threat detection). After prolonged stress, though, the amygdala later atrophies as well.

Not only does stress kill, but it also kills your brain.

Key takeaways:

- Chronic stress can contribute to a higher allostatic load
- Allostatic overload contributes to biological dysregulations
- Biological dysregulations can lead to neurological changes
- Neurological imbalances contribute to mental health disorders, such as PTSD and other mental health vulnerabilities.

Now, here I will summarize some findings from a longitudinal study from Adam and colleagues.[154] In this study, they wanted to see the effect of perceived racial discrimination (PRDs) at different developmental stages and what cumulative effects this would lead to over time. Youth participants were recruited at age 12 and followed for 20 years. They were asked about interpersonal discrimination within the school setting, race-based daily hassles, and racial microaggressions.

Key takeaways from this study:

- Black people were being discriminated against more than White people.
- Greater impacts of PRDs when people were in higher education.
- Black participants had flatter adult diurnal cortisol slopes (hypocortisolism).
- PRDs, which occurred especially in adolescence, would heighten adult risks of hypocortisolism.

The challenges we experience here are that you are more likely to be discriminated against if you are a Black person. There are higher chances of being discriminated against if you decide to challenge the status quo. There are biological consequences to being on the receiving end of racism. And these consequences are especially significant when they occur at the key developmental period of adolescence.

The mental and physical health disparities may then be an accumulation of multigenerational transmission and the experiences of discrimination (regardless of whether it is considered discrimination by White people or not). It is unclear as to how many generations of trauma can be transmitted in this epigenetic format. The members of the Iroquois confederacy, my Native brothers and sisters in Kahnawake, have often

---

[154] Adam, E. K., Heissel, J. A., Zeiders, K. H., Richeson, J. A., Ross, E. C., Ehrlich, K. B., Levy, D.J.,
Kemeny, M., Brodish, A.B., Malanchuk, O. and Peck, S.C., (2015). Developmental histories of perceived racial discrimination and diurnal cortisol profiles in adulthood: A 20-year prospective study.
Psychoneuroendocrinology, 62, 279-291.

spoken about how the decisions made today impact seven generations later.[155] This could be a possibility.

A White Supremacist society cannot easily prioritize mental health or even the physical health of its constituents, knowing that non-White people exist in it. If we ask enough questions about why different racial groups have different health outcomes, we might have to dig deep into the consciousness of a nation founded on colonialism and be very uncomfortable with what we find. The founding of our nations back then indirectly left scars on the population today. It is the maintenance of discrimination in its present form, the need for Black people, and all marginalized people, to be in a state of hypervigilance, to suffer, to internalize it deeply into the nervous system. The racial hierarchy, the gender roles, the homophobic social order are all designed to place a strain on the system of those who do not conform to an ideology of binaries.

IN SUMMARY

The consequences of racism have neurobiological and epigenetic consequences. Because we cannot always discriminate between real and perceived stressors, the brain responds to perceived discrimination as it would to any other prehistoric predator. Because the nervous system seeks homeostasis, allostasis is necessary to invoke our fight or flight responses so that we either normalize or habituate to the hostile environment of White supremacy. The cost of this is allostatic overload, which prompts neurological imbalances, further leaves us vulnerable to stresses in the environment, and leaves us more susceptible to both physical and emotional stressors. Our exposure to stresses, whether post or pre-conception, can impact later generations. This domino effect can ensure the impact of the cycles of violence can self-perpetuate themselves.

I have never been one to believe that there is no way out. Our healing is necessary. I write this, so we understand what is at stake. The act of defeating racism, of recovery from the complexes of trauma, from the socially constructed mental illness that affects us all; this is our act of rebellion. In a world that pushes us toward trauma, shame, and suffering: Recovery is our revolution. Healing is our resistance.

---

[155] Hauptman, L. M. (2008). *Seven generations of Iroquois leadership: The six nations since 1800.* Syracuse University Press.

INTERNALIZED OPPRESSION AND HOMEOSTASIS

For the maintenance of self-esteem and the actualization of the myth of White dominance, the myth of Black inferiority must be internalized. The effects of constant inferiorization also affects our nervous system.

Racial Trauma:

Commonly seen as events of danger, due to real or perceived experiences of racial discrimination.*

Additionally:

- Adversity occurs in both covert and overt ways in the present.
- Experiences are related to historical and multi-generational trauma from the past.
- There is a degree of social acceptance and pervasiveness for this form of trauma.

THE NEUROLOGICAL EFFECTS OF STRESS

The HPA-Axis REGULATES STRESS

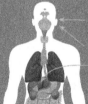

Hypothalamus

Pituitary Gland

Adrenal Glands
(Above kidney)

The HPA-Axis generates CORTISOL

- The process is adaptive when short term *(acute)*.
- BUT it is maladaptive when long term *(chronic)*.

Keep in mind: vulnerabilities to stress may be passed down through generations. So we can inherit the suffering of our ancestors...but remember, we can also inherit their resilience.

EVERY SYSTEM SEEKS HOMEOSTASIS

It does not matter if it is harmful or helpful... homeostasis occurs through allostasis.

Allostasis → is a shift in cardiovascular, metabolic, immune, and central nervous system functioning.

Effects of Allostatic Load[**]
Chronic Stress leads to → Allostatic Load
Allostatic Load leads to → Biological Dysregulation

Biological Dysregulation leads to → Neurological changes

Neurological changes lead to → Vulnerabilities to future stresses

→The system then remains vulnerable to stress

This predisposes an individual to additional emotional, physical, and mental health vulnerabilities... and the cycle continues...

*Comas-Díaz, L., Hall, G. N., & Neville, H. A. (2019). Racial trauma: Theory, research, and healing: Introduction to the special issue. *American Psychologist*, 74(1), 1.
**McEwen, B. S. (2006). Protective and damaging effects of stress mediators: central role of the brain. *Dialogues in clinical neuroscience*, 8(4), 367.

CHAPTER 9:

CARING FOR THE THERAPIST –

MINDFULNESS AND MIRROR NEURONS

Meditation Retreat

I was seated, surrounded by multiple meditators. Some of them were sitting cross-legged; others were sitting upright, assisted by meditation benches. There was a bluish hue in the dark room that covered the numberless other wayward travelers. We came in search of a method to eliminate suffering. We all were practicing a form of meditation called Vipassana.

Although we were not breathing in unison, our paths converged to this place. We decided to take 10 days out of our schedules to look inwards. The rules were strict: no speech would be permitted during this time, no eye contact, no alcohol, no meat or dairy, no physical contact with another person. Male and female meditators were separated for the duration of the retreat.

In such a space, I realized that insights and revelations could arise even without a therapist's prompting. I realized that the body held suffering in its structure, and within each exhalation, a story was released. As I focused, I relieved both the physical and emotional tensions associated with it.

I learned about myself as I sat with my suffering.

When one meditates, they can sit with themselves and receive answers. This silence can be a form of allowing the body and mind to heal. Many times the therapist can suffer from the nature of sitting with another's experience of suffering. Thus, it is important to discuss how we can be more mindful of ourselves, those we share space with, and the organizations we are a part of.

The "Other"

In our professional training as mental health professionals, we are inundated with experiences and conceptualizations of the "other," but never as much relating to the self. We are, in a way, trained to look outside of ourselves for answers and to look out for distress on the outside. While we have manuals and trainings that are designed to conceptualize pain and suffering in others, there is not as much focus on helping the therapist themselves.

This, in a way, may relate to the social prioritization of Whiteness. Authors have explained that conceptual models founded on Eurocentric principles are likely to focus more on the individual than the community they are a part of.[156] The field of psychology has been pressured to be accepted as a science even at the times of its early conception.[157] It could be this drive that relates to why we need to focus more on diagnosing intrapsychic phenomena rather than appreciating the dynamic interaction of interacting with whole human beings, or even the energy of interaction, the mutual exchange between client and clinician.

---

[156] Belgrave, F. Z., & Allison, K. W. (2018). *African American psychology: From Africa to America.* Sage Publications.
[157] Johansson, P. M., & Punzi, E. (2019). Jewishness and psychoanalysis-the relationship to identity, trauma and exile. An interview study. *Jewish Culture and History, 20*(2), 140-152.

But it is designed in this way. Many psychotherapists suffer from the same issue that affects our general society. The dichotomy of White supremacy and Black suffering is reflected in the therapist/client dyad. The expert and the novice. The teacher and the student. The healer and the sufferer. But what if these binaries are also socially constructed? As much as they purport to learn from us, in therapy, we too can be inspired by our clients' triumphs. The lines are not always clearly drawn. As I will discuss here, there are many in the mental health field who are driven to heal but are wounded healers themselves.

Our clinical training emphasizes what we know in our heads rather than what drives us in our hearts. Still, all of this education on its own does not appear to prevent professional misconduct from taking place in our field,[158] so there must be something more to it. There must be a way of developing compassion or at least emphasizing an approach that is considerate before we contribute to the process of dehumanizing that is so deeply ingrained in our society. For this reason, this chapter is dedicated to the preservation of the mental health care worker. The foundational principle relates to mindfulness and the capacity to look inwards. It is necessary to discuss and define mindfulness as a principle and self-care as a necessity for conducting anti-racist psychotherapy.

The Cultivation of Mindfulness

Mindfulness, as a general concept, can be understood as being aware of events as they come to pass. Being mindful involves identifying with the current moment without being influenced by our past experiences or future expectations. The intended result is to achieve a state where we can experience reality as it is, rather than experiencing a reality dictated by our unconscious fears or misconceptions. Kabat-Zinn provides a working definition that describes mindfulness as "the awareness that emerges through paying attention on purpose, in the present moment, and nonjudgmentally to the unfolding of experience moment by moment."[159]

---

[158] Capawana, M. R. (2016). Intimate attractions and sexual misconduct in the therapeutic relationship: Implications for socially just practice. *Cogent Psychology, 3*(1), 1194176.
[159] Kabat-Zinn, J. (2003), Mindfulness-Based Interventions in Context: Past, Present, and Future. *Clinical Psychology: Science and Practice,* 10, 144–156.

Mindfulness-based approaches are inspired by many East Asian religious practices (specifically meditation) and beliefs. While it is designed to aid our work with clients, Kabat-Zinn suggests clinicians themselves should be highly experienced and familiar with mindfulness. It is explained that as one practices meditation, one must practice mindfulness.

The ability to motivate clients toward insight, acceptance, or change is an immutable necessity. However, our clinical effectiveness is a function of our state of mind at a given moment. While our therapeutic interventions and approaches may provide us with words and clinical hypotheses, what goes without saying often speaks the loudest. Here I am referring to the realities of countertransference and transference. Feinstein explains that with these phenomena, the past "lives on as a symbolic representation which unconsciously displaces one's direct experience of the present."[160] Our own specific identities, racial and otherwise, may influence the thoughts of our clients as much as our interventions. Yet the reverse is also true; characteristics of the client can also awaken unconscious reactions or prejudices within the therapist.

Researchers have often discussed the prevalence of racial, ethnic, and religious prejudice in North America.[161] The authors discuss multiple findings that address the reality of systemic racism and how it affects multiple aspects of the lives of marginalized groups. The color of one's skin plays a significant role in the lives of those who are racial minorities. This necessitates the importance of cultural responsiveness among psychotherapists. It is important for clinicians to be aware that we ourselves can augment this sense of marginalization through our own conscious beliefs and latent biases.

Lillis and Hayes further considered how a mindfulness-based approach (e.g., acceptance and commitment therapy) could be used to circumvent unconscious racist or prejudicial sentiments among

---

[160] Feinstein, D. (1990). Transference and countertransference in the here-and-now therapies. *Hakomi Forum*, 1(8), 7-13.
[161] Kucsera, J.V. (2009). *Racial Mindfulness : Exploring the Influence of Mindfulness on Racial Biases* (Doctoral dissertation). Retrieved from UT Electronic Theses and Dissertations.

undergraduate students.[162] They found that participants who were able to improve their ability to recognize the mental processes of judgment and evaluation of others focused less on the content of their thoughts and feelings. The authors explained that what is important is not addressing the negative content, but the "awareness of" and the "relationship to" the negative thoughts. In a way, the intention then is to be cognizant of negative cultural countertransference as it arises, rather than opposing or feeling guilt by its manifestations. Knowing who we are and tending to ourselves allows us to stay healthier and also be better therapists.

The Shared Suffering of Psychotherapy

In our counseling training, regardless of how many years we study, we inevitably come up to that one slide or a couple of slides about self-care. It is rarely the most important part of the presentation. Those few PowerPoint slides we have that relate to self-care in our training professions underestimate the potential damage incurred by burnout and secondary trauma. The experience of vicarious traumatization has negative consequences on a clinician's personal and professional life.[163] Despite the fact that burnout is a real risk for therapists who are exposed to stories of suffering, many of us are often ill-prepared for diving into the abyss of deep suffering that our clients regularly survive and brave through on a daily basis.

As discussed in other chapters, the mind does not easily distinguish between real and perceived stressors. Similarly, when we are witnessing our clients in distress or even while we are listening to their stories, we also become impacted by them. While we have discussed social defeat in rodents elsewhere, there are studies that indicate that for rodents, merely witnessing the social defeat of another rodent can be a significant stressor even without direct exposure.[164] And as this phenomenon occurs in

---

[162] Lillis J., Hayes S.C. (2007). Applying acceptance, mindfulness, and values to the reduction of prejudice: a pilot study. *Behavior modification, 31*(4) , pp. 389-411.
[163] Trippany, R. L., Kress, V. E. W., & Wilcoxon, S. A. (2004). Preventing vicarious trauma: What counselors should know when working with trauma survivors. *Journal of Counseling & development, 82*(1), 31-37.
[164] Warren, B. L., Vialou, V. F., Iñiguez, S. D., Alcantara, L. F., Wright, K. N., Feng, J., ... & Bolaños-Guzmán, C. A. (2013). Neurobiological sequelae of witnessing stressful events in adult mice. *Biological psychiatry, 73*(1), 7-14.

rodents, it also occurs in humans. Isobel and Angus-Leppan discuss "neuro-reciprocity," explaining that the interpersonal dynamic of mental health workers has a bi-directional component.[165]

Neuro-Reciprocity: The Connection Between Patients and Clinicians

Isobel and Angus-Leppan explain this process of neuro-reciprocity by explaining "mirror neurons." They explain that when a person experiences an emotion, there is brain activity in the anterior insula, anterior cingulate cortex, and inferior frontal cortex. If you were to watch this individual experiencing an emotion, the same regions of your brain would also light up. We experience what the other experiences. This process of being empathic with others occurs for better or for worse. While it allows for us to feel joy when others are around, it allows us to also identify with others who are going through hard times. We can "feel" the client's anxiety, depression, and trauma. This form of empathic response causes the clinician to be more susceptible to being vicariously traumatized themselves.

The authors go on to explain that a dissociative response to this process may underlie the vicarious traumatization process. When we are talking to someone who is overactivated, then we too see this and become overactivated. This activates the sympathetic nervous system because we are accessing trauma material. Yet, because we cannot fight, flight, freeze, or fawn during the counseling process (as our clients may not appreciate this), we have to subdue these responses. Here we bring in the parasympathetic nervous system response to attempt to regulate these processes. The therapy then becomes toxic to the provider. With the repeated empathic process of identifying with trauma and attempting to dissociate from it, the accumulation of these allostatic patterns places a strain on the system, leading to the suffering of the health care worker. The more we repeat this process, the more we reduce our ability to compartmentalize the trauma and become disoriented and disconnected from the work.

---

[165] Isobel, S., & Angus-Leppan, G. (2018). Neuro-reciprocity and vicarious trauma in psychiatrists. *Australasian Psychiatry*, *26*(4), 388-390.

Cieslak and colleagues[166] conducted a meta-analysis, where they explained the risks of job burnout and secondary traumatic stressors for those who work with trauma survivors. These secondary stressors are commonly associated with many terms such as vicarious trauma, secondary exposure, indirect exposure to trauma, or even secondary PTSD.

A key factor for job burnout is exhaustion. The researchers explain that although there is debate relating to conceptualizing a one-dimensional definition for job burnout and whether it also comprises cognitive exhaustion or disengagement from work-related tasks of colleagues, it is often related to the structure and demands of the work environment.

Secondary traumatic stress, on the other hand, relates to a broad range of emotional and cognitive changes that appear to resemble individuals who have had actual exposure to traumatic events. The authors cite Bride and colleagues,[167] indicating that there are symptoms that resemble thought intrusions, avoidance of triggers, and heightened levels of physiological arousal.

What is important is that they found that high levels of job burnout and secondary trauma symptoms are likely to co-occur, and that they are higher among professionals who are indirectly exposed to adverse experiences (mental health professionals) and that women are more likely to be affected. The impact of these experiences affects the clinician's general effectiveness and standard of life outside of work.

While my perspective is that the work itself can be hazardous, it is important to take caution. Other researchers see the impact of working with traumatized patients as being over-estimated,[168] instead suggesting

---

[166] Cieslak, R., Shoji, K., Douglas, A., Melville, E., Luszczynska, A., & Benight, C. C. (2014). A meta-analysis of the relationship between job burnout and secondary traumatic stress among workers with indirect exposure to trauma. *Psychological services*, *11*(1), 75.

[167] Bride, B. E., Robinson, M. M., Yegidis, B., & Figley, C. R. (2004). Development and validation of the secondary traumatic stress scale. *Research on social work practice*, *14*(1), 27-35.

[168] Devilly, G. J., Wright, R., & Varker, T. (2009). Vicarious trauma, secondary traumatic stress or simply burnout? Effect of trauma therapy on mental health professionals. *Australian & New Zealand Journal of Psychiatry*, *43*(4), 373-385.

the level of affective distress a clinician will have from working in the trauma field is not just exposure to possibly secondary traumatic events but the workplace itself and other individual factors which may mediate the impacts of vicarious trauma transmission.

It is important to find solutions to change the status quo. Trippany, Kress, and Wilcoxon employ an approach called constructivist self-development theory to provide suggestions for what counselors can do in order to prevent vicarious trauma and other forms of work-related stress.[169] The importance of this is to encourage self-care.

Recommendations include:

- Limiting caseloads—specifically the number of trauma clients a clinician would take on per week;
- Promoting peer supervision where discussions of vicarious trauma, alleviation of countertransference reactions, and shared resources can occur; increasing the responsibility of the agency to decrease vicarious trauma including measures such as supervision, staffing, insurance for personal counseling, and increasing both income and paid vacation for staff;
- Having sufficient trauma-informed training, understanding the impact of adverse childhood events of clients, and how these relate to vicarious trauma;
- Improving personal coping mechanisms, which involves a proper work/life balance, physical activity, including activities that increase the clinician's personal tolerance level; and
- Spirituality, or developing one's deeper sense of meaning and connection to the world around them.

---

[169] Trippany, R. L., Kress, V. E. W., & Wilcoxon, S. A. (2004). Preventing vicarious trauma: What counselors should know when working with trauma survivors. *Journal of Counseling & development, 82*(1), 31-37.

The Responsibility of Organizations

Therapists are not immune to the effects of being indirectly exposed to trauma from their clients. Hence, the organizations which employ them have a responsibility to protect them as well.

Bell, Kulkarni, and Dalton outline several structures that agencies and other organizations can implement to ensure adequate care for their staff.[170]

Organizational Culture: Normalizing and anticipating the effects of trauma on employees can naturally reduce shame and allow clinicians to take care of themselves. Self-care can be a part of what is regularly discussed in staff meetings and even a part of the mission statement. No effort at preserving staff is unwelcome.

Workload: Variation of client presentations in one's caseload can reduce the chance of workers getting overburdened and developing a negative worldview. Additional variation of responsibilities can even relate to giving workers the chance to engage in activism. This cultivates a sense of purpose and reduces the negative effects of trauma work.

Work Environment: Workers must be entitled to a safe workspace without fear of entering or leaving the building. Having meaningful items such as pictures of loved ones in worker's workspaces, inspirational quotes in hallways, posters of scenic landscapes in staff areas, are agency actions that "model the importance of the personal in the professional."

Education: The authors explain that the ability to name trauma allows for a conscious response toward vicarious trauma. Training settings have an obligation to inform interns and therapists in training about the risks of secondary trauma. Workshops that discuss these events allow for

---

[170] Bell, H., Kulkarni, S., & Dalton, L. (2003). Organizational prevention of vicarious trauma. *Families in society, 84*(4), 463-470.

therapists to feel more competent when addressing any foreseeable obstacles.

Group Support: The importance of groups cannot be overstated. Group activities can range from celebrating birthdays to critical incident debriefing. Although there are always risks in groups to regress to "group think" or other problematic re-enactments, established boundaries, roles, and explicit expectations can often provide the necessary support.

Supervision: One of the most effective forms of managing difficulties is by sharing one's story with a supportive other. Regular supervision can be a reliable solace from an unending stream of challenging clients. An emphasis on safety and skill development is essential. Separating supervision from evaluation can allow junior therapists to learn from mistakes and refine progress.

Resources for Self-Care: Once again, peer support can be an important means of mutual assistance between colleagues. It is also possible to have regularly scheduled activities for structured stress management workshops. Additionally, encouraging staff members to share self-care methods is not only cost-effective but cultivates a culture of caring for one another.

IN SUMMARY

The first step in undoing oppression is to heal that which is internal to ourselves. Many of us who come to the field are trauma survivors. This necessitates the use of self-care and the courage of mindfulness, being capable of being present, and self-monitoring so that we reduce the chance of negative countertransference in session. But above and beyond countertransference is the risk inherent in our capacity for neuro-reciprocity; our gift for empathy carries the risk for burnout and secondary traumatic stressors. It is important not only for those who undertake the task of assisting others in seeking healing themselves, but it is a moral responsibility of the agencies that employ trauma therapists to adequately prepare their workers for the undertaking of trauma reprocessing. Monitoring caseloads, granting access to training, providing adequate wages, promoting adequate supervision, and encouraging a self-care culture, all of these things in turn increase our effectiveness with our clients. Let us be willing to take the same medicine we prescribe to others, self-awareness and self-compassion.

MINDFULNESS AND SELF-CARE

In the field of mental health, we must prioritize self-care and the preservation of the therapist. As we care for others, we must care for ourselves.

Mindfulness

An awareness that is purposeful, present-oriented and non-judgmental. It can be practiced and developed.

Although some see it as a relaxation technique, it is meant to be an approach that works towards the elimination of suffering.

Neuro-receptivity

Through mirror neurons, we have an innate capacity to connect, relate, and identify with the experience of others.

Empathy helps us to connect with clients.

- But we "dissociate" to avoid fully identifying with them.
- We suppress our own emotional and physical responses.
- And the repetition of this leads to secondary trauma symptoms.

Organizations have an ethical responsibility to protect their therapists

Individual Factors

Proper work/life balance
Physical activity
Cultivation of mindfulness
Having a sense of meaning
Getting your own therapist

Organizational Factors

Encourage peer support
Reduce shame about secondary trauma
Provide adequate wages/vacation
Provide trauma-informed training
Provide appropriate supervision for staff

Self-care is important, but organizations must support it. It takes individuals to start it, but it takes a community to maintain it. Everyone must do their part to create a culture of resilience and harmony.

PART FOUR:
AN ANTI-RACIST APPROACH TO
PSYCHOTHERAPY

CHAPTER 10:

THE INTEGRATIVE

PSYCHOTHERAPEUTIC STANCE

Shadowing

"You're not understanding me," I watched through the two-way mirror as a student therapist attempted to convince the client. The mirror neurons were firing; despite the student and the client disagreeing, they both looked like they were on the verge of jumping out of their seats.

"But I do understand you; it's just that you have to leave him!"

I shook my head and turned slightly away from the plexiglass. I was shadowing a fellow student in training. We were taking turns meeting with clients and practicing the essential therapeutic skills which would help us as therapists-in-training build rapport and connection with clients. Except, in this case, it was not happening. Everyone knows what it is like to see that a disaster is imminent; it's hard to watch because you know what's coming.

"Leave him? I'll leave you!" the client said, then leaped up, stamped their feet emphatically, and slammed the door. Those of us observing went to debrief with the student and tried to cheer him up. We consoled, we hypothesized. But what was interesting was the explanation given to him by one of the more experienced students.

"Yeah, that client was borderline after all; she was just showing a lot of resistance."

I responded, "Borderline? Resistance? I don't understand." My questioning was seen as a lack of experience. Disdain crept from their lips and their glances. My status needed to be delegitimized through microaggression. How could anyone not know that the problem was the client's resistance? Or the stigma toward a mental health diagnosis? How dare I assume that the student could do anything wrong.

All forms of therapy are more complex than they seem, but we must avoid stigmatizing and putting pride before progress. We must learn to be more compassionate and reduce blame and other therapist-initiated obstacles for success. In this chapter, we will consider common factors as well as psychological recommendations from an Africentric perspective.

What Actually Makes Therapy Work?

In earlier generations of psychotherapists and mental health practitioners, there were frequently different "camps" and arguments relating to which style of psychotherapy was superior. Would it be those who relied on cognitions, those who relied on behaviors, the perspective of the therapist, or that of the client? As varied as the people who exist on this planet, there is such a large degree of different psychotherapeutic modalities.

But what is consistently found is that, regardless of the type of therapy that takes place, what frequently accounts for the greatest degree of clinical success is not always the clinical approach but what are called common factors. Common factors have often been cited as one of the most important determining factors of clinical success in systemic therapies such as family interventions,[171] couple therapy,[172] and across individual therapies.[173] We consider common factors because, while there are many different theoretical perspectives and backgrounds, it is challenging to demonstrate one model's complete superiority over another because studies repeatedly demonstrate that other psychotherapies claim equal success.

Common Factors

In defining an anti-racist psychotherapy that is already integrative in its nature, it is then important to not get caught up with claiming superiority with a model intended to confront White supremacy. But it is still necessary to discuss certain traits that can enhance therapy or at least allow it to have some use to the potential client. Grencavage and Norcross' literature review found that, across all categories, what was shared among disciplines was the need for establishing a proper therapeutic alliance, opportunities for catharsis, acquiring and practicing new skills, positive engagement by the client, therapist qualities, and an ecological rationale for the process of change.[174] While there was an importance placed on change processes and encouraging them during the therapeutic session, the most important commonality between all psychotherapies was the development of a collaborative therapeutic alliance.

Although that research is several decades old, the conclusions have stood the test of time consistently. Wampold similarly finds that we can decipher what some of these common factors are through meta-analysis and use of the contextual model.[175] The author begins by elucidating three essential paths to therapeutic success:

---

[171] Sprenkle, D. H., & Blow, A. J. (2004). Common factors and our sacred models. *Journal of marital and family therapy, 30*(2), 113-129.
[172] Davis, S. D., Lebow, J. L., & Sprenkle, D. H. (2012). Common factors of change in couple therapy. *Behavior therapy, 43*(1), 36-48.
[173] Grencavage, L. M., & Norcross, J. C. (1990). Where are the commonalities among the therapeutic common factors?. *Professional psychology: Research and practice, 21*(5), 372.
[174] Ibid.
[175] Wampold, B. E. (2015). How important are the common factors in psychotherapy? An update. *World Psychiatry, 14*(3), 270-277.

- a social relationship/human connection where an empathic person tends to another;

- an explanation for suffering and viable treatment offered by the therapist, and;

- a relationship where the therapist elicits healthy client actions.

Wampold continues his findings, explaining that evidence for common factors are the components for a therapeutic alliance: empathy, warmth, and a caring environment; expectations and rationale for treatment; characteristics of the therapist; as well as cultural adaptation of psychotherapeutic treatments.

Provided that a therapy is delivered with a structure by a therapist who cares, and the client is engaged in activities that augment their well-being, there does not appear to be significant differences between different therapeutic orientations. Adhering to standard protocols is highly recommended and at times essential for some special populations.[176][177] But what is also clear is that rigidly adhering to a structure damages therapeutic alliance and increases client resistance.[178]

It is for this reason, that it is possible for any therapy to be anti-racist and, while I may provide recommendations and approaches, I am limited by my experience and knowledge of what works for my client populations. Any other person's therapeutic approach will also be expected to be a confluence of their personal experiences, professional training, and opportunity for education.

While there is not one specific aspect to be added into a therapy to make it better than another, there are some nice-to-haves that have been helpful for the range of client populations that I have worked with, including BIPOC, LGBTQ, those suffering from substance abuse and

---

[176] Lock, J. & Le Grange, D. (2015). *Treatment manual for anorexia nervosa: A family-based approach*. Guilford Publications.

[177] Leeds, A. M. (2016). *A guide to the standard EMDR therapy protocols for clinicians, supervisors, and consultants*. Springer Publishing Company. 2nd edition. New York: Springer Publishing Company.

[178] Wampold, B. E. (2015). How important are the common factors in psychotherapy? An update. *World Psychiatry, 14*(3), 270-277.

eating disorders, clients in youth protection, immigrants, domestic violence survivors/offenders, and many others. When one reflects on their clinical training, we cannot help but recognize that it is not only our trainers who have taught us but the clients too, who often spur the realization that this takes skills. Although I give credence to the many thought leaders and giants in the field who came before me, I am forever indebted to my clients who have always been my best teachers and who taught me I need to step my game up.

Africentric Psychology

The following is a summary of a significant chapter by Belgrave and Allison, who wrote *African American Psychology: From Africa to America*.[179] The authors describe, in their second chapter, some notable and important facets of Africentric psychology. These are perspectives that influence this branch of psychology that are derived from the worldview of individuals of African descent. Names of psychologists and theorists who contribute to our understanding of Africentric psychology are Joseph White, Wade Nobles, Na'im Akbar, Daudi Ajani Ya Azibo, Kobi K. K. Kambon, and Linda James Myers.

Fundamental Africentric Dimensions

The following is a summary of Belgrave and Allison's discussion of African worldview dimensions. It is explained that many of these values are not unique only to Africans but may also exist in other collectivist cultures like Latinos, Native Americans, Asians, and other non-Western groups.

Spirituality

The authors describe this fundamental principle as having a belief in a force greater than the individual. In the African culture, spirituality exists both inside and outside of religion as opposed to Western conceptions. The highest fulfillment in spirituality is harmony as opposed to materialism, which focuses on acquiring goods and services. The authors explain that

---

[179] Belgrave, F. Z., & Allison, K. W. (2018). *African American Psychology: From Africa to America*. Sage Publications.

more African Americans are likely to report religious beliefs than their European American compatriots.

Collectivism

This dimension encourages the idea of interdependence and mutual cooperation. The importance of significant others, family, and community are central—collectivism clashes with individualism. The accumulation of material goods is not seen as a priority in comparison to the maintained harmony of interpersonal relationships. Family is paramount; even "fictive kin" are apparent in collectivist cultures where people with no biological relation can still be seen as being "uncles" or "aunties."

Time Orientation

In Western cultures, the focus on time is toward the future, while in African cultures, the past, present, and future carry equal weight. Rather than being a linear process, time is seen as a cyclical, flexible process. This can lead Africans to be more present-oriented, while the Western perspective emphasizes prediction and measurement. The authors use the term "colored people time" to describe this flexibility with time. Over time, I noticed it was not just my family who had this flexible perspective relating to time. I have often observed it in Native communities, Asian, Indian, and even when I traveled to Lebanon.

Orality

In the West, there is a preference toward what is written, while African society would traditionally transmit knowledge orally. It is the transmission of oral knowledge that allowed for the preservation of African traditions and perspectives to enslaved Africans during the genocide and kidnapping of the treacherous diaspora.

Sensitivity to Affect and Emotion

This relates to a capacity to recognize the emotional states of others while having one's own emotions recognized by the other. There is meant to be an association between one's affect and their actions, a synchronicity between one's emotions and behavior.

Verve and Rhythm

There is a preference for movement and variability, but there are multiple ways of teaching and learning. Didactic means of instruction can also be varied; rather than only visual stimuli from the top-down, there can also be the involvement of creative means of instruction from the bottom-up.

Balance and Harmony with Nature

As opposed to the perspective of needing to master and control nature, one finds their place within the scope of existence. The African worldview lends itself toward the perspective that if there is a spiritual imbalance, there may well be physical, emotional, or mental imbalance.

The authors quote Grills, who explains additional concepts that are important for the therapist and the therapeutic process.[180]

- *Ma'at*
  - The cardinal principle that manages balance and order. It encompasses truth, justice, compassion, harmony, balance, reciprocity, and order. As we practice these virtues, they become more prominent within us.

- *Maafa*
  - The term used to describe the chattel slavery process initiated by Europeans toward Africans. The goal of Maafa was humiliation, social defeat, and the complete destruction of the people of Africa.

- **Veneration of the Person**
  - All living beings are worthy of dignity and respect. The lives of the living are interconnected with those who have passed. Every life carries a sacred value.

---

[180] Grills, C. T. (2004). African psychology. In R. L. Jones (Ed.), *Black psychology* (4th ed.). Hampton, VA: Cobb & Henry.

- **Spiritness**

  - Refers to the wholeness of the individual. It suggests that all individuals are in possession of a valid mind, soul, drive, and passion. There is an acknowledgment that the spirit is both real and metaphoric.

- **Human authenticity**

  - There is a drive toward approaching life from a place of sincerity and authenticity. Without authenticity, a lack of trust develops, which promotes hypervigilance, distrust, and the feeling of a constant threat to survival.

- **Inclusive metaphysical epistemology**

  - Knowledge from both affective and cognitive realms of interpretation are equally valid. There is an understanding that reality is not limited to just the five senses. Rational logic is not the only form of knowledge.

- *Sankofa*

  - A word from the Twi language of Ghana which represents that before one advances forward, they must be aware of what has already passed. Knowledge from past historical events helps in understanding present events. It represents the need to return to African roots, culture, and identity for guidance.

One can perhaps see that, although these approaches may be considered Africentric, there are similarities to other cultures, specifically toward the cultural origins and traditions of mindfulness. While there are a variety of different cultures in the world, many of the most popular psychotherapies that I am aware of have been created from a Eurocentric model/mindset. Because there is likely not 100% homogeneity within any sample, there may be cases where some of the above, though relating to an African worldview, may also be amenable to European or American clients or research participants. There may even be a way of boosting the effectiveness of Western models of psychotherapy by revising or infusing them with the principles listed above.

IN SUMMARY

Because the question occurs every so often, it is sometimes necessary to revisit the question of which therapeutic modality is the greatest or most effective. This question is, of course, rooted in a system of what is superior versus what is inferior. What every psychotherapist must strive toward is the importance of pragmatism rather than social proof. But in many of these comparisons between approaches, the jury is out and the common factors come out on top. Therapeutic alliance, empathy, and acknowledging the client as a person rather than an object can go a long way. But if clients' problems occur in a Eurocentric environment with Eurocentric expectations, it may be possible that the answers lie outside of that environment. The Africentric models discussed above include a conceptualization of spirituality and a sense of balance that is separate from religion and a focus on a collective identity that is in harmony with nature. What is interesting is that many African Americans who have been separated from their African origins due to the *Maafa* for generations appear to respond well to Africentric approaches despite having a different "culture" from outside of the African continent.[181] Perhaps we are all closer to one another than we think.

---

[181] Belgrave, F. Z., & Allison, K. W. (2018). *African American Psychology: From Africa to America*. Sage Publications.

THE INTEGRATIVE
PSYCHOTHERAPEUTIC STANCE

Although there are many types of therapeutic modalities, we must discuss what makes them effective.

COMMON FACTORS

Here are the most important predictors for clinical success. A collaborative therapeutic alliance is the most significant.*

 Therapeutic Alliance: Collaboration between client and clinician.

 Opportunities for Growth: Clients can see change.

 Empathy, Warmth and a Caring Environment: Feeling supported.

 Skill Acquisition and Development: Learning and practicing.

 Setting Expectations and Rationale for Treatment: Being reasonable.

 Cultural Adaptation of Treatment: Making adjustments for the client's perspective.

 Therapist Characteristics: Interpersonal skills, capacity to form alliances, constant skill development, etc.

FUNDAMENTAL AFRICENTRIC PSYCHOLOGICAL DIMENSIONS

There are also some aspects of Africentric Psychology that are important to think about when working cross-racially or with clients of African descent.**

 Spirituality: There is a force greater than just the individual.

 Collectivism: Interdependence and mutual cooperation.

 Time Orientation: Being "present-oriented" or even "flexible" with time.

 Orality: Knowledge transfer through the spoken word is valued.

 Verve and Rhythm: Multiple ways of teaching and learning.

 Balance and Harmony with Nature: One finds their place within the world; there is an inter-connectivity to all things.

*Grencavage, L. M., & Norcross, J. C. (1990). Where are the commonalities among the therapeutic common factors?. *Professional psychology: Research and practice*, 21(5), 372.

*Wampold, B. E. (2015). How important are the common factors in psychotherapy? An update. *World Psychiatry*, 14(3), 270-277.

**Belgrave, F. Z., & Allison, K. W. (2018). *African American Psychology: From Africa to America*. Sage Publications.

CHAPTER 11:

THE ANTI-RACIST EMDR APPROACH

Awesomeness

"Thank you for helping me to find my awesomeness," the client said. Before then, we had been working for a year and had little progress using traditional methods of treatment. Several years of adverse childhood experiences left the White, non-binary client in an altered state of hypervigilance, depression, and a host of medical issues. A borderline personality disorder diagnosis led to additional challenges and resistance.

At our group practice, we exhausted all of the options for addiction treatment centers that we could have possibly send them to. It was seemingly hopeless because, as much as I had attempted to engage them cognitively with writing exercises and talk therapy, there were constant states of relapse.

The approach we decided to use instead was Eye Movement Desensitization and Reprocessing (EMDR) therapy. Although it was not easy, it still seemed to advance something that the other talk therapies, hospitalizations, treatment center admissions, and police officer restraints were unhelpful in accomplishing. It helped get to the root of the trauma, which was underlying the addiction.

Though I reflect on it now, feeling sad that they had to go through such re-traumatizing experiences because of our lack of resources, systemic barriers, and the general misunderstanding the public has toward complex trauma and addiction, we did everything we could to save them.

I am forever grateful that they did not give in to their depression. Therefore, I was a witness to them, saving their own life. Tears streamed down both of our faces as I left the group practice. It was an exchange of gifts. Their gift was that they found their "awesomeness," something that they already had. My gift was that I learned that all people can recover from trauma with the right context, support, and therapeutic technology.

For us to assist those who suffer deeply, we must at times, accompany them during times of great difficulty. EMDR therapy is a way of being able to help some people who otherwise are not as responsive to other forms of therapy. In this chapter, I will discuss ways of utilizing EMDR therapy from an anti-racist perspective.

How Developmental Trauma Impacts Us

In my practice, I have found that EMDR therapy is highly effective in assisting clients who suffer from complex trauma. It is a structured approach that follows eight phases and is a three-pronged approach designed to address past traumatic events, present issues of disturbance, and future behaviors.[182] Although it is highly structured, it is still possible to make adjustments and improvements to it, such as following an anti-racist framework and still maintaining the integrity of the model. By following integrative conceptualizations and adding compassionate adjustments to each phase, we can promote a more collaborative and supportive journey toward reprocessing trauma.

Prior to using the EMDR psychotherapeutic approach, it is essential

---

[182] EMDRIA. (n.d.) *Experiencing EMDR Therapy.* https://www.emdria.org/about-emdr-therapy/experiencing-emdr-therapy/

to understand why we would use it. It is my hope to inform and raise consciousness around this often misunderstood but life-changing psychotherapeutic modality.

Neurobiology may help to inform the response that an individual may have to stressors. As previously stated, chronic stressors trigger the hypothalamic-pituitary-adrenal axis (HPA axis), which moderates the release of cortisol.[183] Chronic over-activation of stress response systems contributes to wear and tear on the body, which is called allostatic load.[184] Elevated allostatic loads contribute to further biological dysfunction, leaving an individual even more susceptible to stress-borne illnesses and mental health dysregulation.[185]

Del Giudice, Ellis, and Shirtcliff explain that one's calibration of a stress response is highly dependent on experiences during developmental years.[186] The social identity of an individual may contribute to their susceptibility or vulnerability to different kinds of stresses. For example, while most individuals can be affected by early childhood rejection (even if this may not typically be seen as traumatic), Del Giudice and colleagues cite Stroud, Salovey, and Epel,[187] explaining that there is typically higher HPA axis activation patterns for women in situations relating to social rejection. While there may be evolutionary explanations for this gendered response, it is important to know that how the individual identifies and how the world identifies them impacts their susceptibility to the effects of stress. This may explain why there are mental health disparities that exist even between racial groups.[188]

---

[183] Berger, M., & Sarnyai, Z. (2015). "More than skin deep": stress neurobiology and mental health consequences of racial discrimination. *Stress, 18*(1), 1-10.

[184] McEwen, B. S. (1998). Stress, adaptation, and disease: Allostasis and allostatic load. *Annals of the New York academy of sciences, 840*(1), 33-44.

[185] McEwen, B. S. (2006). Protective and damaging effects of stress mediators: central role of the brain. *Dialogues in clinical neuroscience, 8*(4), 367.

[186] Del Giudice, M., Ellis, B. J., & Shirtcliff, E. A. (2011). The adaptive calibration model of stress responsivity. *Neuroscience & Biobehavioral Reviews, 35*(7), 1562-1592.

[187] Stroud, L. R., Salovey, P., & Epel, E. S. (2002). Sex differences in stress responses: social rejection versus achievement stress. *Biological psychiatry, 52*(4), 318-327.

[188] Berger, M., & Sarnyai, Z. (2015). "More than skin deep": stress neurobiology and mental health consequences of racial discrimination. *Stress, 18*(1), 1-10.

Events that relate to early attachment disruptions are essential to consider from an EMDR perspective. Di Corcia and Tronick[189] explain that, based on the Everyday Stress and Resilience hypothesis, when mothers are unable to attend to their infant children's essential needs, the developing child may later lack the essential coping skills which could have come from their mother's reparatory sensitivity. Regulation from one's caregiver contributes to the infant's later ability to self-regulate. The relationship between a child and their mother can influence the child's propensity to manage later stresses in their life: "for an infant, this can consist of coping with micro-stressors, the ubiquitous disruptions in the typical flow of communication within the mother-infant dyad."[190]

If we are met with challenges from the environment during our early childhood experiences, whether from our family of origin or the environment itself, there is a heightened possibility that an individual will then experience difficulties coping with everyday micro-stressors, especially with regards to separation or rejection from attachment figures.

Taylor and Stanton explained that individuals with mental health disorders might lack appropriate coping resources. It is the lack of these resources which leads to difficulties.[191] The mental health disorder an individual has is not only exacerbated by the lack of resources at the key developmental ages, but it is also the inability to cope with present stressors because of a lack of resources, which were not learned at those earlier states.

The Multigenerational Cycle of Suffering

Repetti, Taylor, and Seeman explain that it is not unlikely that individuals raised in "risky families" would be likely to rely on health-

---

[189] Di Corcia, J. A., & Tronick, E. D. (2011). Quotidian resilience: Exploring mechanisms that drive resilience from a perspective of everyday stress and coping. *Neuroscience & Biobehavioral Reviews, 35*(7), 1593-1602.
[190] Ibid.
[191] Taylor, S. E., & Stanton, A. L. (2007). Coping resources, coping processes, and mental health. *Annu. Rev. Clin. Psychol., 3*, 377-401.

threatening behaviors such as alcohol consumption and drug abuse.[192] A client's drug and alcohol abuse can often be a means of "compensating for deficiencies in social and emotional development, as well as a self-medication process whereby [youth] manage the biological dysregulations produced or exacerbated by risky families."

It is summarized that families characterized by aggression and neglect increase risks for the following:

- threats to the safety of the children;
- increased contributions to allostatic loads for children raised in these environments;
- difficulty providing self-regulation skills for children; and
- a higher likelihood for children to develop behavioral problems and substance abuse issues.

The cycle is that those children who develop these behavioral issues and substance abuse issues are likely to continue this pattern unless the traumatic origins which preceded it have been sufficiently processed. The cycle of suffering replicates itself through a person's family history, yet also through their genealogy. If we question why a specific individual exhibits a maladaptive behavior, we must consider the context that allowed for it or promotes it. For this reason, the EMDR phases are well suited to consider both past, present, and future and move clients who have complex presentations beyond the routine day to day management of symptoms and toward a greater sense of resilience and self-worth.

Reprocessing Our Trauma With EMDR Therapy

EMDR has been shown to be especially promising with regards to PTSD.[193][194] But in addition to being helpful with PTSD, it is also effective

---

[192] Repetti, R. L., Taylor, S. E., & Seeman, T. E. (2002). Risky families: Family social environments and the mental and physical health of offspring. *Psychological Bulletin, 128*, 330-366.

[193] Mosquera, D., Leeds, A. M., & Gonzalez, A. (2014). Application of EMDR therapy for borderline personality disorder. *Journal of EMDR Practice and Research, 8*(2), 74-89.

[194] World Health Organization. (2013, August 6). *WHO releases guidance on mental health care after trauma.* Retrieved December 20, 2020 from

in cases where an individual may have experienced repeated exposure to childhood neglect and early adverse childhood experiences including, but not limited to, borderline personality disorder. Seliga mentions that when accounting for clients who have PTSD, BPD, or both diagnoses co-morbid, it appears as if EMDR may demonstrate higher rates of treatment efficacy than the more "popular" or treatment as usual psychotherapies.[195]

The theoretical underpinnings of EMDR are based on the Adaptive Information Processing model.[196] This model explains both pathology and therapeutic outcomes within the EMDR framework.[197] Individuals internally process incoming information by assimilating new experiences into previously established neural networks of memories. When this internal information processing system is working adequately, it will metabolize new experiences and incorporate them into previously held memory networks allowing integration and the ability to adapt to new experiences.

Psychopathology occurs when new experiences cannot be metabolized. This can be brought about when the individual is confronted with traumatogenic events. Brown and Shapiro explain that these experiences come in the form of either "small-t" or "large-T" traumas. Large-T traumas could be seen as PTSD inducing events such as childhood sexual abuse, whereas small-t traumas may be events that may not be as acutely distressing but which may still leave marks of distress on a person. An example of a small-t trauma could be the type of invalidating environment that leads an individual with BPD to experience childhood

---

https://www.who.int/mediacentre/news/releases/2013/trauma_mental_health_20130806/en/

[195] Seliga, M. (2009). Empirically supported treatment interventions for clients with posttraumatic stress disorder and comorbid borderline personality disorder: A critical review. *Where Reflection & Practice Meet The Changing Nature of Social Work: Towards Global Practice.*

[196] Brown, S., & Shapiro, F. (2006). EMDR in the treatment of borderline personality disorder. *Clinical Case Studies, 5*(5), 403-420.

[197] Solomon, R. M., & Shapiro, F. (2008). EMDR and the adaptive information processing model potential mechanisms of change. *Journal of EMDR practice and Research, 2*(4), 315-325.

neglect or abandonment.[198]

These traumatic memories become stored in a dysfunctional manner and are prevented from successfully integrating with adaptive or self-regulating neural networks. It is hypothesized that when memories are encoded in this unprocessed, distressing, and dysregulating form, "the original perceptions can continue to be triggered by a variety of internal and external stimuli, resulting in inappropriate emotional, cognitive, and behavioral reactions, as well as overt symptoms (e.g., high anxiety, nightmares, intrusive thoughts)."[199] Maladaptive behaviors, cognitions, or personality characteristics result from unprocessed, dysfunctional memories, cognitions, and events.

It is for this reason that EMDR may be best suited for racial trauma. Because racial trauma is not just the specific event in itself but is likely an accumulation of traumatic events that have affected an individual's sense of self, sense of identity, and present-day sense of security. It is imperative to utilize an approach that can target and reprocess this stored traumatic material in a unique way.

The Eight Phases of EMDR

EMDR is composed of eight different phases:

1. History Taking and Treatment Planning
2. Preparation
3. Assessment
4. Desensitization
5. Installation
6. Body Scan
7. Closure
8. Re-evaluation

The first two phases may occur over the span of several sessions, while

---

[198] Brüne, M. (2016). Borderline Personality Disorder Why 'fast and furious'? *Evolution, medicine, and public health, 2016*(1), 52-66.

[199] Solomon, R. M., & Shapiro, F. (2008). EMDR and the adaptive information processing model potential mechanisms of change. *Journal of EMDR practice and Research, 2*(4), 315-325.

phases three to eight are when the EMDR bilateral stimulation procedure for reprocessing traumatic events transpires. The first two phases are especially important, and they will be discussed here.

EMDR Phases One and Two

In the first phase of history taking and treatment planning, it is especially important to provide questionnaires that screen and evaluate risks for dissociation. Stabilization is an essential first step in many complex trauma cases. When clinicians are inappropriately trained, the risk of retraumatization to the client from prematurely beginning treatment can occur. For this reason, there are a variety of questionnaires and assessment tools that EMDR practitioners are trained to use. While the DES-II is helpful as an initial screening tool, the MID-60 has been shown to demonstrate valid and reliable results and is much more comprehensive in scope than the DES-II.[200]

There are instances when a therapist may modulate between phases one and two, and they would be wise to do so. Discussing material that relates to key developmental traumas can likely be destabilizing for clients who are ill-prepared. For this reason, it is best practice to teach self-soothing and emotion regulation strategies early on to not only introduce the client to bilateral stimulation and other means of body-mind regulation but also to build confidence. The preparation phase is important for building confidence because we can teach the client that they have what it takes to manage and self-soothe their own emotions.

Genogram

The use of the genogram is common among couple and family therapists but is especially helpful for the history-taking process. A genogram is a graphical representation of one's family system.[201] Members of one's family are represented by different shapes and graphical symbols, much like a family tree. The use of this is that, in addition to

---

[200] Kate, M. A., Jamieson, G., Dorahy, M. J., & Middleton, W. (2020). Measuring Dissociative Symptoms and Experiences in an Australian College Sample Using a Short Version of the Multidimensional Inventory of Dissociation. *J Trauma Dissociation*, 1-23.
[201] McGoldrick, M., Gerson, R., & Petry, S. S. (2008). *Genograms: Assessment and intervention*. WW Norton & Company.

collecting information about relevant family members, it is imperative to demonstrate to the client that at least some degree of their problems have been inherited. Cultural legacies, addictions, gender roles, and patterns of violence become clarified through this process. This is done in a way that is meant to raise consciousness and promote understanding, especially when it is explained in the context of individuals coping in either adaptive or maladaptive ways. The genogram has been a valuable tool in itself to assist clients in recognizing that once unconscious patterns are made conscious, we have the choice to either maintain or change them.

As mentioned above, because discussing family history and other historical issues may reveal touchstone events, it is especially important to teach resources and methods of managing challenging emotional states or vulnerable ego states. This is done by first devoting time toward stabilization and emotion regulation techniques and/or visualizations. Each time a client becomes triggered, it is expected of the therapist to reinforce that the client is gaining the capacity to self-regulate and improve their ability to recover.

Trauma History

Prior to beginning trauma reprocessing, the client begins to record the trauma history. The trauma history is a chronological list of events that have happened throughout the client's lifespan. Specific instructions are given so that the client does not recount the history of each specific event. This is done in part because of the sake of time and also because of the risk of re-experiencing without containment. Once again, client safety is paramount, and so while listing the trauma history items, the clinician checks in with the client after specifically challenging events are listed.

The importance of consent is taken seriously. If the client requests to focus on resources or emotion regulation, they can interrupt the process at any time to focus on grounding. This process of co-creating the treatment process and trauma history also allows for clients to avoid giving any identifiable details about the traumatic event itself. There have been many individuals I have worked with where I was unaware of what the traumatic event was because the client had too much shame or did not feel ready to discuss. Because EMDR is not a typical talk therapy, it is perfectly valid for a client to not share major details and still gain complete resolution of their issue.

Intergenerational Racial Trauma

For racial trauma, clinicians must be comfortable asking questions that relate to instances of microaggression, homophobia, gendered violence, and/or traumatic issues that occurred before the client was born. Any event which precedes the client's birth that still affects them to this day may potentially leave its marks on the client's nervous system and thus be fair game for reprocessing. Even if a client may stare at you strangely when you ask about events before their life, second-generation trauma is a real phenomenon. Not only can second-generation traumatic events be reported from descendants of holocaust survivors, but it can also be reprocessed using EMDR.[202]

In my practice, I have done so with Indian residential school survivors, descendants of survivors of the *Maafa,* and others whose ancestors were lost to civil war or other genocidal events. All pathogenic memories carry not only the dysfunctional association to a past event but the internalized negative belief about oneself or one's "collective." Although it is not always necessary (and not always requested by Black, White, or other racial minority clients), reprocessing events relating to the transgressions or victimizations of previous generations can reduce shame, inspire pride, and set the stage to reprocess other trauma history events which may require a base level of self-worth and purpose. Resolving key racial trauma events improves one's general sense of self-esteem, one's general level of self-compassion, and a heightened appreciation for their cultural group, racial identity, and the collective whole.

EMDR Phases Three to Eight

For the remaining phases, the reprocessing of traumatic memories occurs using dual attention, either by using bilateral stimulation or

---

[202] Nickerson, M. (2017). *Cultural competence and healing culturally based trauma with EMDR therapy: Innovative strategies and protocols.* Springer Publishing Company

utilizing complex tasks that tax working memory.[203][204] As stated earlier, when the distorted format that the traumatic memory is recorded in is presented with these conflicting forms of stimulation, the memory becomes reconsolidated. Rather than the client re-experiencing the trauma as if they were there, they can, at times, move fairly quickly toward feeling states of "distance" from the memory and, in many cases, "compassion" toward themselves and those involved.

The assessment phase selects and prepares the traumatic memory target for bilateral stimulation or the working memory taxation procedure. The desensitization procedure is meant to reduce the subjective measurement of disturbance of the traumatic event as well as reduce the integrity of the internalized negative belief one holds about themselves relating to the event (e.g., "I am worthless"). The Installation phase is then meant to install a positive or adaptive belief relating to the trauma (e.g., "I am a proud Black woman"). The body scan is meant to mindfully notice that all parts of the body agree with the newfound adaptive belief, and then closure is meant to contain the session and prepare the client toward finishing the session and continuing on their day. Re-evaluation is intended to verify during the following session if the client managed to successfully complete the reprocessing. In my experience, if during re-evaluation, the client reported no residual discomfort relating to the memory, the traumatic event would then be resolved, and most often, would no longer be a bother to the client.

It is clear that, because of the speed and efficiency of EMDR, there have been many detractors and skeptics, but this undue cynicism toward the approach does not appear to get in the way of its results, as stated by other authors as well.[205]

---

[203] de Jongh, A., Ernst, R., Marques, L., & Hornsveld, H. (2013). The impact of eye movements and tones on disturbing memories involving PTSD and other mental disorders. *Journal of Behavior Therapy and Experimental Psychiatry, 44*(4), 477-483.
[204] Matthijssen, S. J., van Schie, K., & van den Hout, M. A. (2018). The Effect of modality specific interference on working memory in recalling aversive auditory and visual memories. *Cognition and Emotion.*
[205] van der Kolk, B. A. (1996). *The body keeps score: Approaches to the psychobiology of posttraumatic stress disorder.* In B. A. van der Kolk, A. C. McFarlane, & L. Weisaeth

IN SUMMARY

It is important for us to understand that the mental health disorder does not occur in a vacuum. Of course, though trauma and stress are not the only precursors to mental illness, as it is understood that there can be genetic predispositions to some disorders,[206] it is still relevant for us to conceptualize some of the most challenging diagnoses as perhaps being more than just the client's fate and/or their permanent label. Many disorders are not only a difficulty coping, but the lack of the opportunity given to learn to cope due to a challenging home environment. The adaptive information processing model posits that we are all prone to healing and adaptive behavior so long as we can target what has been dysfunctionally learned. We invoke either bilateral stimulation or working memory taxation methods while following the process of therapeutic memory reconsolidation principles. But once more, there are ways of using these structured approaches while still coming from a place of compassion. Anti-racist EMDR means using every opportunity to empower the client in a collaborative and authentic way without victim-blaming or pathologizing the client's journey toward recovery.

(Eds.), *Traumatic stress: The effects of overwhelming experience on mind, body, and society* (pp. 214–241). The Guilford Press.

[206] American Psychiatric Association. (2013). *Diagnostic and statistical manual of mental disorders: DSM-5*. Washington, D.C: American Psychiatric Association.

THE ANTI-RACIST EMDR APPROACH

Chronic stress initiates a cascade of events

Chronic Stress → HPA-axis → Cortisol Release → Allostatic Overload → Biological dysregulation → Increased vulnerability

The timing matters

Early developmental trauma + the inability of the caregiver to soothe the child = a child who will not know how to cope with stress

Mental health stresses occur largely as a result of...

Maladaptive methods of coping

Insufficient resources

EMDR Therapy is designed to address the client's past, present, and future adversity. The 8 phases of the EMDR protocol were developed by Dr. Francine Shapiro*.

History taking and treatment planning

Understand present and past context of distress.

Preparation

Teach culturally relevant skills of self-soothing, elicit client's potential for coping.

Assessment

The set up for desensitization.

Desensitization

Use of bilateral stimulation and/or working memory taxation.**

Reduces maladaptive memory associations.

5. Installation

Reinforces adaptive memory network connections.

6. Body Scan

Allows for all "parts" of the body to accept the new positive cognition.

7. Closure

Ends the session using Flash technique or other resources as necessary.

8. Reevaluation

Occurs at the beginning of each session. Verifies that changes have maintained.

*Shapiro, F. (2017). *Eye movement desensitization and reprocessing (EMDR) therapy: Basic principles, protocols, and procedures.* Guilford Publications.
**de Jongh, A., Ernst, R., Marques, L., & Hornsveld, H. (2013). The impact of eye movements and tones on disturbing memories involving PTSD and other mental disorders. *Journal of Behavior Therapy and Experimental Psychiatry,* 44(4), 477–483.
**Matthijssen, S. J., van Schie, K., & van den Hout, M. A. (2018). The Effect of modality specific interference on working memory in recalling aversive auditory and visual memories. *Cognition and Emotion.*

CHAPTER 12:

AUXILIARY STRATEGIES FOR CLIENT

SELF-CARE

Group Facilitation

I remember it like it was yesterday. On my first day, I was nervous working as a group therapy facilitator. I was younger then, co-facilitating alongside a White woman who was older but as nervous as I was. We were both student interns hoping that the court-mandated men who would barge in would be understanding and kind toward our naive learning process. Well, unfortunately, they weren't.

They sat in a circle after we took their attendance, and they paid their fee for participation. I tried to break the awkwardness by greeting the men. They all appeared twice my age and twice my size.

"What are you studyin'," one of them gnarled out from under his beard.

"I'm studying social work," I cheerfully responded.

Another man, whose muscles appeared to make him resemble a statue of pure violence, glared at me and blurted out to the whole group, "Social worker? Well, I don't *like* social workers."

I felt my heart drop.

The clients were not there voluntarily, and they were not ready to hear counseling advice from a young budding therapist. All of them were Black. So, while I knew that these people were seen as "criminals" and labeled as violent or oppressive, there was something valid to the idea of systemic racism and the fact that, in a White-dominated country, many of the people who I worked with were people of color and, specifically, immigrants. I could not relate with them based on our past, I faltered many times but tried as best as I could to relate, and slowly but surely, I realized it.

Our work necessarily involved discussing what it meant to be a man, what it meant to be Black, and what it meant to be accused and branded as a violent Black male stereotype. This could not occur from the White co-facilitator, who might not have the same level of awareness or social justice orientation. It needed to come from a place of compassion and slight, but not too much identification. I regularly brought in aspects of mindfulness in discussion and tried as best as I could to delicately dance between empathy while confronting patriarchal and anti-social personalities. It was challenging and rewarding.

In our final session, a man who seemingly appeared to be made out of tattoos smiled at me, "You know, we were wrong about you."

I thanked him and breathed a sigh of relief.

The well-sculpted man jumped up out of his seat, beaming with a smile, saying, "I like these meetings man, it always feels like church!"

We all laughed. I also felt changed from our interactions. Although it wasn't the gospel, group therapy had become a place where there was a confession of sins, an acknowledgment of faults, and a purification for all of us involved.

Group therapy is often a complex process but sometimes the entire group contributes to each group member's well-being.. Individual therapy may not always have the advantage of the group, but there is always a way of allying with the client so that they also take responsibility for their own healing. Methods of helping to motivate the client to participate in their own journey towards recovery are essential.

The Empathic Self

The work we did together in that group was very different from what happened in the other cohort, where no discussion on identity beyond masculinity occurred. The experience of the "man" is different from the experience of both the "White man" and the "Black man." We need to have the courage to bring race into the picture, but only when we ourselves are comfortable confronting our own racial prejudices and hang-ups.

And while these individuals were labeled by society as "criminals," I learned that I got nowhere by trying to label them as such in session. If their series of adverse childhood events had been exchanged with mine, I would have been in their seat in the circle, and they would have been in mine. Even outside of the stigmatized categories of domestic violence, addictions, and eating disorders, we must be cautious with labeling and victim-blaming. Rather than victim-blaming, we conceptualize the individual as more than their specific diagnosis when coming from a trauma-informed perspective. It is no longer sensical to define a person as a "schizophrenic" or a "borderline," it is more that we describe people as "having" the symptoms rather than "being" the symptom. Rather than saying that someone is "anorexic," it is more realistic to say that a person has "anorexia nervosa" as a diagnosis. This implies they have it and can potentially stop having it. People are more than their diagnoses.

All people are constantly seeking to adapt, and, in some cases, the mental health disorder is a maladaptive means of coping with interpersonal stresses. Interpersonal stresses are mediated by one's family, society, political, and cultural forces. Certain mental health disorders are culture-bound and are more likely to occur in some groups rather than others. An example of this is depression, which can be seen as a culture-bound syndrome in the West. Depression is not a universal or transcultural concept and is highly influenced by American or European cultural norms and beliefs.[207] The presentation and diagnostic criteria of "depression" in a Canadian person may be very different than in a Malaysian, which may differ from someone from Burkina Faso. The prevalence of anorexia nervosa cannot be the same in all countries that do not share the same ideas of what constitutes a "beautiful" or "thin" or "fit" person. The impact of our societal norms and political views can influence our physical health (as the numbers of people who died from COVID-19 in different countries reveals), but these norms may also relate to our mental health.

While there are commonalities between all people, every individual is different. For this reason, I provide my clients with a multitude of different strategies so that they can customize their self-care. The therapist/client dynamic can be oppressive or pathological if there are not aspects of empowerment embedded into it. This means that the client assumes a degree of leadership and responsibility for their own healing, and the therapist assumes a more supportive role by providing the requisite structure and context for recovery.

In this chapter, I seek to present some auxiliary strategies and techniques which help to empower the client both within and outside of therapy. This is done so that the client is capable of challenging the passive label of client, but also feeling as if they have a place in their therapy process. The client is both the healer and the healed, while the therapist is only there to set the context and witness the spiritual event in its glory.

Rationale for Mobilizing the Client's Self-Healing

While there are general principles to follow, it is also essential to include Miller and Rollnick's principles for motivational interviewing (MI).[208] This is not a technique or even a general model of psychotherapy but a general model of communication that is designed to encourage change.[209] It is brief but is very helpful for working with individuals who have ambivalence concerning the presenting problem, which brings them

---

[207] Dowrick, C. (2013). Depression as a culture-bound syndrome: implications for primary care. *The British Journal of General Practice*, *63*(610), 229.
[208] Miller, W. R., & Rollnick, S. (2012). *Motivational interviewing: Helping people change*. Guilford press.
[209] Miller, W. R., & Rollnick, S. (2009). Ten things that motivational interviewing is not. *Behavioural and cognitive psychotherapy*, *37*(2), 129-140.

to therapy. Because most clients are in a state of ambivalence about whether they wish to continue the problem (maintain what is familiar) or change the problem (brave the great unknown), the principles of motivational interviewing are also essential. MI has common principles that resemble what was discussed in earlier chapters: express empathy, support efficacy, develop discrepancy, roll with resistance. All of these are important in anti-racist psychotherapy.

There are two essential principles to consider in MI; one is to acknowledge and recognize that ambivalence can occur in sessions. As one of my mentors, Tom Caplan, used to say while we were working with "involuntary" or court-mandated domestic violence offenders, "There is no such thing as a 'voluntary client' because no one really wants their problem." The problem is that secondary gain is real. Many people have a problem because there is an upside to the downside. A problem only maintains itself if there is a motivation for keeping homeostasis. Even in cases when a person does something undesirable like substance abuse, which, on the outset, is undesirable for a person to maintain and promotes negative consequences, it is important to know that there is something that is gained from it. Developing a discrepancy between where the client is and where they want to go is essential for people who may be locked in their self-persecutory socially constructed patterns of goal restriction.

And the other essential principle is that resistance in therapy cannot just exist from the client. It is a dynamic between both the therapist and the client. "The least desirable situation, from the standpoint of evoking change, is for the counselor to advocate for change while the client argues against it."[210] Resistance occurs for a variety of reasons: some of which involves the therapist moving too fast for the client, the client having discrepant goals from the therapist, and many other manifestations. What is important to understand is that resistance is a process that can emerge from the therapist themselves. It is the responsibility of the therapist to

---

[210] Miller W. R., Rollnick, S. (2002). *Motivational Interviewing: Preparing People for Change*. New York: Guilford Press, p.39.

identify resistance and "roll with it," redirecting and re-framing resistance as a means of helping the client attain their goals.

Knowing that ambivalence occurs naturally and that resistance can be navigated necessitates skills and approaches that strategically address this. The client is expected to encounter obstacles outside of therapy. They will need skills they can use on their own both within the therapy context and their own personal life.

There are self-care frameworks/strategies that can assist in potentiating EMDR and can be used as self-care, such as cognitive writing strategies and the emotional freedom technique.

Cognitive Writing Strategies

David Burns wrote a book which I believe is the definitive example of "bibliotherapy," in that an individual who would read *Feeling Good: The New Mood Therapy*[211] would have a set of skills that could help to support any standard psychotherapy but also to provide strategies which a client could use to enhance their own well-being in cases where therapy may not be available. Many of the strategies in the book are inspired by the cognitive-behavioral psychotherapeutic approach and specifically targeting what are called "cognitive distortions." Writing about these distortions (which we all possess to some degree) and providing disconfirming evidence or writing out an empathic response to them is a way of self-soothing the mind.

Bibliotherapy is defined as a form of treatment where one would use writing to manage one's own mental health challenges.[212] Meta-analysis has shown that bibliotherapy demonstrates great outcomes when compared to individual psychotherapy for depression.[213] While writing

---

[211] Burns, D. D. (1980). *Feeling good: The new mood therapy*. New York: New American Library.
[212] Yuan, S., Zhou, X., Zhang, Y., Zhang, H., Pu, J., Yang, L., Liu L., Jiang, X., & Xie, P. (2018). Comparative efficacy and acceptability of bibliotherapy for depression and anxiety disorders in children and adolescents: a meta-analysis of randomized clinical trials. *Neuropsychiatric disease and treatment, 14*, 353.
[213] Gregory, R. J., Schwer Canning, S., Lee, T. W., & Wise, J. C. (2004). Cognitive Bibliotherapy for Depression: A Meta-Analysis. *Professional Psychology: Research and Practice, 35*(3), 275.

exercises can be helpful in assisting adolescents who struggle with depression, it may not be as effective with all children who suffer from mental health challenges.[214] The lack of effectiveness of writing exercises with many populations may be due to difficulties in sustaining motivation. We all know that completing homework assignments, especially during childhood, requires some degree of discipline. But even as adults, these cognitive exercises require willpower especially when we are experiencing the stresses of day-to-day living.

It is for this reason that it is necessary to pair writing assignments with the psychotherapeutic context. Writing exercises need not be long or complicated because there is a chance that a client may not complete them. What has been especially helpful in my practice is assigning "Five grateful things." Clients are instructed to take up writing a journal and to write anything they like, but the journal must not be limited to negative topics or complaints. They are also to practice writing at least five things that they were grateful for during the day. If asked for examples, it is important to be vague and also to suggest that they include both important and non-important things in their list. In some cases, being vague can promote self-discovery and encourage the client's leadership capacity outside of the therapy session.

What is important for this exercise is not whether it was completed or not, but more about the self-directed effort toward emotion regulation and the client's general experience. Although it is a cognitive strategy, there is still a soothing that occurs in the body. What was their somatic experience before, during, and after? What did they notice change about their mood in the next few days? Did they have any revelations or new means of interacting with others? Writing in this way provides an endless number of possibilities for discussion. One may find that, with experience, writing about an event with the right intention can gradually elicit dynamic perspectives and the potential to reframe one's own narrative.

---

[214] Yuan, S., Zhou, X., Zhang, Y., Zhang, H., Pu, J., Yang, L., Liu L., Jiang, X., & Xie, P. (2018). Comparative efficacy and acceptability of bibliotherapy for depression and anxiety disorders in children and adolescents: a meta-analysis of randomized clinical trials. *Neuropsychiatric disease and treatment, 14*, 353.

It is important to review any homework assignment provided to a client. If they took the time to complete it, then we must take the time to look it over, but not with the intention of correcting it. The intention is always to help the client to see that they can learn about themselves. Even if one does not complete the activity, this is a communication in itself; it may signify that they see writing exercises as "lame" (as one of my adolescent clients articulately responded), or they may feel that there has not been much to be grateful for. It may also be that the client forgot to complete the assignment. All answers assist in either helping the client to find a means of coping or providing an opportunity to discover what may be more helpful for them. For this reason, integrative therapists must be trained in multiple approaches and avoid being one-trick ponies.

Emotional Freedom Technique (EFT)

EFT is an acupressure-based self-care procedure taught to the client that provides immediate and surprisingly effective assistance for a variety of different emotional and physical ailments. EFT is not to be confused with emotion-focused therapy, a completely different psychotherapy approach that is also effective for couples and families. EFT was developed by Gary Craig, and an explanation along with instructional videos can be found on his website at https://emofree.com by clicking on the section marked "Gold Standard EFT Tapping Tutorial." Since developing this approach, he has focused more on an upgraded approach called Optimal EFT, but the original version will be discussed here.

Although this may not resemble traditional talk therapy either, as there are different acupressure points that both the therapist and client tap on themselves, EFT is an evidence-based treatment for a variety of issues. In addition to being helpful for college students who suffer from depression,[215] meta-analysis has demonstrated remarkable results for veterans who suffer from PTSD and CPTSD.[216] Researchers have found

---

[215] Church, D., De Asis, M. A., & Brooks, A. J. (2012). Brief group intervention using Emotional Freedom Techniques for depression in college students: A randomized controlled trial. *Depression research and treatment, 2012.*
[216] Church, D., Stern, S., Boath, E., Stewart, A., Feinstein, D., & Clond, M. (2017). Emotional freedom techniques to treat posttraumatic stress disorder in veterans: review of

that EFT reduces PTSD symptoms with a diverse population from refugees to combat veterans within 10 or fewer sessions, with sustained benefits at least six months after treatment for more than 80% of participants.[217]

EFT is helpful because both the client and the therapist engage in tapping their own acupressure points in unison. Because it is a self-care technique that both the therapist and client are engaging in, perhaps there is a function of mirror neurons that helps to calm the client and assist the client's capacity to stabilize themselves. There is a call and response approach that involves the therapist instructing the client to focus on tapping on specific points and repeat certain phrases. The client follows and reduces the intensity of their symptoms for both emotional and physical pain symptoms rapidly and effectively.

IN SUMMARY

While this list is by no means exhaustive, it is important to know that there are multiple strategies that can be used to potentiate EMDR and other forms of psychotherapy. MI is important for addressing ambivalence and strategies for targeting secondary gain. Some individuals may not always "want" to get better despite being in therapy, so it is essential to find ways of improving motivation when confronting suffering. Cognitive writing strategies have a long history. For many, writing about experiences offers a fresh perspective on them. In between sessions reflecting on what they are grateful for helps orient clients to the present and allows them to see what resources, big or small, they still have. EFT is helpful not only for stabilization and emotion regulation in session but can also be used by clients externally to assist with managing their emotions in response to challenging situations.

When we are conscious of what maintains homeostasis, resistance can no longer be unconscious. When we can write about our experience, we can recreate our experience. When we have the necessary tools to self-soothe, self-regulate, and co-regulate, we can change the course of our lives.

---

the evidence, survey of practitioners, and proposed clinical guidelines. *The Permanente Journal, 21.*

[217] Sebastian, B., & Nelms, J. (2017). The effectiveness of Emotional Freedom Techniques in the treatment of posttraumatic stress disorder: A meta-analysis. *Explore, 13*(1), 16-25.

AUXILIARY STRATEGIES FOR CLIENT EMPOWERMENT

There is a need to motivate and empower the client to heal themselves. This allows them to see that although they might have the problem, they can also have the solution.

SELF-CARE STRATEGIES

Lessons from Motivational Interviewing*

- **Resistance** is located, not within the client, but within the dynamic between the client and the therapist.

- **Ambivalence** is to be expected even when the presenting problem threatens the client's safety, livelihood or well-being.

Cognitive Writing Strategies

Writing helps us gain new perspectives on present-day stresses. Writing can be used to:

- Encourage motivation for recovery.

- Rewrite and redefine our own narratives.

- Record statements of gratitude to see the positive in the present.

EFT Tapping Points

- Top of the Head
- Between the Eyebrows
- Side of the Eye
- Under the Eye
- Under the Nose
- Under the Mouth
- Collar Bone
- Side of Palm
- Under Arm

Emotional Freedom Technique (EFT)

A self-applied, acupressure-based approach that helps with depression, PTSD, CPTSD populations.** EFT is useful because it:

- Assists in self-care and emotion regulation.

- Helps to potentiate other therapies.

- Improves our awareness of body, emotion, and spiritual resources.

The full protocol is available on
https://emofree.com/eft-tutorial/

*Miller, W. R., & Rollnick, S. (2012). *Motivational interviewing: Helping people change*. New York: Guilford press.
**Church, D., De Asis, M. A., & Brooks, A. J. (2012). Brief group intervention using Emotional Freedom Techniques for depression in college students: A randomized controlled trial. *Depression research and treatment*, 2012
**Sebastian, B., & Nelms, J. (2017). The effectiveness of Emotional Freedom Techniques in the treatment of posttraumatic stress disorder: A meta-analysis. *Explore*, 13(1), 16-25.

CHAPTER 13:

MECHANISMS OF ACTION

Efficiency

"On a scale of zero to ten, how intense is the sadness?" I asked. "Ten," she said.

Tears were running down her face, and we needed to try something beyond just talking about it.

"Where do you feel it in the body now?"

She looked downwards and said, "In my stomach."

"Alright, notice that," I said.

The client was then instructed to notice a specific point in the room, to keep her eyes directed there while listening to music in her headphones, and focusing on the feeling in her stomach. She was to remain mindfully focused while I sat with presence and conviction, holding space for her. She confronted her suffering. At first, she trembled and pulled more tissues from the tissue box right beside her, seeming to lose hope, but she continued. She wiped tears from her blue eyes, clutching the tissues in her hand. Though she was re-experiencing the memory of a challenging past, she was also in a supportive, present environment.

We sat together in silence.

As she continued to listen to the music and continued to maintain her gaze on the left side of her visual field, her breathing began to normalize. The redness in her face receded. She let out a sigh of relief. She was reorienting to the body, reorienting to the present, and now carrying a smile.

"Zero to ten?" I asked.

She paused, reflected, and responded, "It's a… two? You've gotta be kidding me, David!"

She busted out laughing. I could not help but laugh too. We had been working on this early attachment injury with other methods and could not seem to reduce it. The client gained hope that day; it was the first time in a long time that she could genuinely laugh and smile. She proceeded to bring her distress down to zero and maybe even beyond that.

In just one session with this modality, we covered a lot of ground. Strangely enough, I would never know what connections she actually made. She worked it out on her own. There was something highly efficient that was occurring, and the connections were made without my input. It was not necessary for me to give her the answer because she already had the answers within.

"Hey," she said while waving her finger. "If I'm the one who did all the work, then shouldn't you be the one paying for this session?"

I raised my shoulders and jokingly sighed, "C'mon, now you know that's not in the contract, right?"

We laughed some more. Her traumatic event was reprocessed. The pathogenic memory was reconsolidated. She was able to smile again.

Recovering from trauma is not easy, but there are ways of empowering the client throughout the process. In this chapter, it will be necessary to address some of the nuts and bolts that underlie why these approaches work and more deeply explore some of the efficient approaches we have available.

Advancing Our Technology

There is a certain reluctance or unwillingness to believe that psychotherapy can take place in a shorter amount of sessions. This may be because many of us have been brought up to believe that work is a function of time and what we see occurring. We are skeptical when something takes place faster than we expect it to because of conditioning. Food takes time to prepare, books take time to read, and transportation is not instant. We doubt when certain processes occur faster than expected. Psychotherapy is no stranger to skepticism, and healthy skepticism is useful. However, let us not allow our skepticism to become cynicism. Our limitations are based on our misconceptions and perhaps in need of a software update.

Technology is ever advancing. Computers are much more advanced now than they were 10 years ago, and much more advanced than they were 10 years before then. Technology will continue to advance even if most laypeople do not fully comprehend how to write a line of code. But even if we ourselves are not software engineers, we do not doubt the usefulness of computers. Even though we do not see cloud servers, we still have (relative) trust in their capacity to preserve our data. Hence, just because we do not understand the complexities of our neural networks and the brain's innate capacity to heal, we must not doubt the capabilities of our neural supercomputers just because the technology is advanced or not yet fully understood.

The following will describe some neuroscience informed means of treating pathogenic memories. I will begin with some proposed mechanisms of action for EMDR therapy and a short discussion of Brainspotting and the Flash Technique..

Mechanisms of Action

While the EM part of EMDR stands for eye movement, there are several ways of using bilateral stimulation and several more hypothesized mechanisms of action. We say hypothesized because several include a variety of explanations relating to REM sleep, mindfulness, working memory, and other neurological explanations. For an in-depth description of each, see Leeds' *A Guide to the Standard EMDR Therapy Protocols for*

Clinicians, Supervisors, and Consultants textbook.[218] While there is no unanimous agreement for what causes the change that leads to the reprocessing of pathogenic memories, we know more about what initiates it. Leeds cites decades of research and explains that the primary mediator is based on "dual attention," which is defined as "a state in which consciousness is in balance and where attention can fluidly shift between current sensory perceptions and relevant memory networks." Dual attention relates to the pairing of bilateral stimulation and accessing one's activated targeted memory network. Doing so allows clients to desensitize the target memory (and its corresponding negative cognition) and then reprocess the traumatic material so the client can acquire a more adaptive positive cognition.

While there are several hypothesized mechanisms of action, Leeds suggests that the orienting (or investigatory) response (OR) gives us one of the earliest explanations for how EMDR therapy works and is often used to explain how people benefit from it. I second that here, in part because I primarily use auditory and tactile forms of bilateral stimulation when conducting EMDR therapy, and clients can still reprocess traumas effectively. Specifically, I use the "butterfly hug" technique developed by Lucina Artigas. A summary of Leeds' explanation is provided here: Leeds quotes Jeffries and Davis, explaining that eye movements involve both an alerting response and an investigatory response.[219] He then refers to Siegel, explaining that the repetitive pairings of an orientation response (e.g., focusing on the negative memory) and sub-cortical appraisal of safety (e.g., being in the therapists' office or a video conference meeting during session) leads to a gradual habituation and nervous system response of synchronization, safety, and homeostasis.[220] The orienting reflex has been cited as a mechanism of action for EMDR therapy

---

[218] Leeds, A. M. (2016). *A guide to the standard EMDR therapy protocols for clinicians, supervisors, and consultants*. Springer Publishing Company. 2nd edition. New York: Springer Publishing Company.

[219] Jeffries, F. W., & Davis, P. (2013). What is the role of eye movements in eye movement desensitization and reprocessing (EMDR) for post-traumatic stress disorder (PTSD)? A review. *Behavioural and cognitive psychotherapy*, *41*(3), 290.

[220] Siegel, D. J. (2012). *The developing mind: How relationships and the brain interact to shape who we are (2nd ed.)*. New York, NY: Guilford Press.

by many researchers. [221][222][223][224][225] Furthermore, the "disconfirming knowledge" of safety provided by the orienting reflex appears to reflect what Ecker and colleagues explain in the memory and therapeutic reconsolidation process.[226] This "prediction error" of being safe in the present results in the accessed memory being altered, which then leads to a permanent change once this memory is reconsolidated with the updated information.[227]

Resource Development and Installation

There are certain clients who are insufficiently resourced or have high levels of developmental trauma. In these instances, reprocessing may not always work as efficiently as possible. The preparation phase of EMDR therapy provides clients with the opportunity to learn skills or resources that can assist them. Some resources that are commonly used involve pairing structured and guided visualizations with the client in the form of the calm place or light stream technique.[228] However, there is a form of resourcing that is essential in EMDR therapy. It is called the Resource Development and Installation (RDI). It is a guided visualization based method of ego strengthening that assists in stabilization to decrease shame, depersonalization, and several other therapy interfering behaviors inside

---

[221] MacCulloch, M. J., & Feldman, P. (1996). Eye movement desensitisation treatment utilises the positive visceral element of the investigatory reflex to inhibit the memories of post-traumatic stress disorder: a theoretical analysis. *The British Journal of Psychiatry, 169*(5), 571-579.

[222] Lipke, H. (1992). *Manual for the teaching of Shapiro's EMDR in the treatment of combat related PTSD.* Pacific Grove, CA: EMDR Institute.

[223] Lipke, H. (1999). *EMDR and psychotherapy integration: Theoretical and clinical suggestions with focus on traumatic stress.* Boca Raton, FL: CRC Press.

[224] Armstrong, M. S., & Vaughan, K. (1996). An orienting response model of eye movement desensitization. *Journal of Behavior Therapy and Experimental Psychiatry, 27*(1), 21-32.

[225] Armstrong, N., & Vaughan, K. (1994, June). *An orienting response model for EMDR.* Paper presented at the meeting of the New South Wales Behaviour Therapy Interest Group, Sydney, Australia.

[226] Ecker, B., Ticic, R., & Hulley, L. (2012). *Unlocking the emotional brain: Eliminating symptoms at their roots using memory reconsolidation.* Routledge.

[227] Manfield, P., Lovett, J., Engel, L., & Manfield, D. (2017). Use of the flash technique in EMDR therapy: Four case examples. *Journal of EMDR Practice and Research, 11*(4), 195-205.

[228] Shapiro, F. (2017). *Eye movement desensitization and reprocessing (EMDR) therapy: Basic principles, protocols, and procedures.* Guilford Publications.

and outside of sessions.[229] Leeds conceptualizes resources as being elicited from three categories: memories of mastery, relational resources, and symbols. With the careful selection of appropriate resources, we can assist clients in improving their present-day functioning and helping them in reprocessing many of the challenging childhood traumatic events at the foundation of their present-day disturbances.

I would also like to discuss additional resources that assist clients who suffer from severely disturbed states and cannot readily access calm place visualizations or even use RDI to reduce the intensity of trauma reprocessing. For these cases, it is recommended to use psychotherapeutic interventions that are well suited for addressing the needs of highly dissociated and severely traumatized clients who are supported in a psychotherapeutic setting. They are two of my personal favorites and have been used with various clients who suffer from eating disorders, substance abuse issues, complex PTSD dissociative issues, and other challenges.

Brainspotting

Brainspotting (BSP) is defined as a psychotherapeutic approach that is highly effective for distressing events and was developed by Dr. David Grand. It can be used for either trauma processing or resource development.[230] The foundation of BSP is the attunement between client and therapist.[231] Masson, Bernoussi, and Moukouta explain that the process involves locating specific eye positions in the client's visual field related to "brainspots."[232] Brainspots appear to correspond to specific neurological responses to the targeted distressing event. Focusing on a specific brainspot with sustained mindful awareness leads to sub-cortical

[229] Leeds, A. M. (2016). *A guide to the standard EMDR therapy protocols for clinicians, supervisors, and consultants*. Springer Publishing Company. 2nd edition. New York: Springer Publishing Company

[230] Grand, D. (2013). *Brainspotting: The revolutionary new therapy for rapid and effective change*. Sounds True.

[231] Corrigan, F., & Grand, D. (2013). Brainspotting: Recruiting the midbrain for accessing and healing sensorimotor memories of traumatic activation. *Medical Hypotheses, 80*(6), 759-766.

[232] Masson, J., Bernoussi, A., & Moukouta, C. S. (2017). Brainspotting Therapy: About a Bataclan Victim. *Global Journal of Health Science, 9*(7).

cerebral activity that efficiently resolves traumatic events, performance-related impediments, and various other distressing situations.[233]

Although there may be a lack of robust research studies compared to other, more established psychotherapies,[234] BSP shows great promise as an emerging therapy. BSP appears to demonstrate comparable outcomes to EMDR therapy. Hildebrand, Grand, and Stemmler have discussed that BSP provides similar effectiveness rates as EMDR therapy in populations impacted by trauma.[235] Almeida, Macêdo, and Sousa cited research by Fuzikawa[236] where they explain that study participants found a 90% reduction in PTSD symptoms.[237] A similar reduction was reported in PTSD symptoms in an additional study.[238] There are numerous other case studies and anecdotal results[239] that demonstrate the effectiveness of BSP with diverse populations, which range from a traumatized survivor of a terrorist attack[240] to a dissociative childhood sexual abuse trauma case.[241]

---

[233] Grand, D. (2013). *Brainspotting: The revolutionary new therapy for rapid and effective change.* Sounds True.

[234] Gurda, K. (2015). Emerging trauma therapies: Critical analysis and discussion of three novel approaches. *Journal of Aggression, Maltreatment & Trauma, 24*(7), 773-793.

[235] Hildebrand, A., Grand, D., & Stemmler, M. (2017). Brainspotting–the efficacy of a new therapy approach for the treatment of Posttraumatic Stress Disorder in comparison to Eye Movement Desensitization and Reprocessing. *Mediterranean Journal of Clinical Psychology, 5*(1).

[236] Fuzikawa, C. (2015). Brainspotting: uma nova abordagem psicoterápica para o tratamento do trauma. *Revista Debates em Psiquiatria, 3*, 26-30. Retrieved from http://abpbrasil.websiteseguro.com/portal/wp-content/upload/rdp_15/03/RDP_3_2015_geral1.pdf

[237] Almeida, A. K., Macêdo, S. C. G. D. M., & Sousa, M. B. C. D. (2019). A systematic review of somatic intervention treatments in PTSD: Does Somatic Experiencing® (SE®) have the potential to be a suitable choice? *Estudos de Psicologia (Natal), 24*(3), 237-246.

[238] Hildebrand A., Grand, D., Stemmler, M., (n.d.) A preliminary study of the efficacy of Brainspotting –a new therapy for the treatment of Posttraumatic Stress Disorder. *Journal for Psychotraumatology, Psychotherapy Science and Psychological Medicin.* Retrieved from: https://brainspotting.com/wp-content/uploads/2018/02/Hildebrand-Grand-and-Stemmler-2014-Jrnl-Psyctrau-PsyctherSci-Pysclgcl-Med20.pdf

[239] Grand, D. (2013). Brainspotting: The revolutionary new therapy for rapid and effective change. Sounds True.

[240] Masson, J., Bernoussi, A., & Moukouta, C. S. (2017). Brainspotting Therapy: About a Bataclan Victim. *Global Journal of Health Science, 9*(7).

[241] Patrícia F.M., José F.P., de F and Marcelo M (2015) Persistent Genital Arousal Disorder as a Dissociative Trauma Related Condition Treated with Brainspotting – A Successful Case Report *Int J Sch Cog Psychol S1*: 002 Retrieved from https://brainspotting.com/wp-content/uploads/2018/02/Ferreira-Mattos-et-al-2015-IntlJrnlofSchandCogPsych-CaseRpt-S1.pdf

As with other brain-based approaches, it is essential that the client notice the specific issue and acknowledge the somatic experience. The emotional intensity and physical discomfort which accompany recalling traumatic events is termed as "activation" and is recorded on a one to ten "Subjective Unit of Disturbance Scale" (SUDS), which was originally created by Joseph Wolpe. The SUDS is a way of the client giving a subjective report of how much disturbance they are detecting. The number zero represents the absence of disturbance, and the number 10 represents the highest level possible.

Grand explains that once the level of SUDS is determined and the body sensation is identified, we are then able to locate the brainspot. The brainspot represents a point of activation on the client's visual field, which is the access point for reprocessing trauma. There is no need for the therapist or client to discuss or converse about the issue, and, once again, with this form of brain-based therapy, the therapist can be "blind" to the target. The therapist does not need to know the content for the client to fully resolve the issue. Processing occurs so long as the client remains attuned, the therapist is present, and the brainspot and activation are kept in awareness.

As the client focuses on the brainspot while being aware of their body sensations, they are also provided with bilateral music, which alternatively pans from left to right in their headphones. The type of music can vary from smooth and soft music to sounds of nature and other recordings of ambient soundtracks.

Although there are similarities to EMDR in that the eyes are used, BSP is less constrained to specific protocols and places a higher focus on what is called "focused" mindfulness.[242] There is a greater need for the therapist to be in a state of stillness and hold space for the client, while the client is instructed to attend to attune to their inner state and accept uncertainty. Doing so allows the client to rapidly and efficiently resolve troubling material. The combination of mindful observation, therapeutic presence, and soothing music appears to work favorably for even the most disturbed

---

[242] Grand, D. (2013). *Brainspotting: The revolutionary new therapy for rapid and effective change*. Sounds True.

clients. However, there are some cases when even those with high levels of distress require additional support.

When attempting to locate or focus on a brainspot, clients can sometimes demonstrate reflexes that are initiated at a subcortical level. These involuntary and automatic responses can resemble squinting, nostril-flaring, facial tics, coughs, or swallowing, yet blinking is one of the most commonly observed. Corrigan and Grand explain that blinking is related to alterations in brain functioning and information processing. The orienting of one's gaze toward a fixed location activates the capacity for healing deep-seated emotional pains at an efficient and deep level.[243] This act of orienting, focusing on brainspots associated with past trauma, while in a present-day context that allows for a sense of safety, appears to allow a person to gradually feel calm even when recalling distressing events. Once again, this allows for disconfirming the past reality and reorienting to the present.

Flash Technique

Manfield and colleagues describe the Flash Technique (FT) as a tool to assist in the preparation phase for EMDR.[244] Flash Technique is still under development; hence even the hypothesized mechanisms of action provided in this cited article are likely to be updated within the months that follow publication of this book. FT is an approach that appears to reduce experiences of distress quickly and efficiently. It is an additional method that appears to have drawn its inspiration from EMDR therapy in that it also involves bilateral stimulation and eye blinking. Examples of FT are available at the following URL: https://flashtechnique.com/

It is not unusual to see clients who use FT recount stories that leave them smiling and beaming, though seconds before they described situations of terror or significant distress. For this reason, in addition to using it at the second phase of preparation at the outset, it is especially

---

[243] Corrigan, F., & Grand, D. (2013). Brainspotting: Recruiting the midbrain for accessing and healing sensorimotor memories of traumatic activation. *Medical Hypotheses*, *80*(6), 759-766.

[244] Manfield, P., Lovett, J., Engel, L., & Manfield, D. (2017). Use of the flash technique in EMDR therapy: Four case examples. *Journal of EMDR Practice and Research*, *11*(4), 195-205.

ANTI-RACIST PSYCHOTHERAPY

useful during the seventh EMDR phase of closure. This ensures that the client leaves the session in a grounded and positive state. I have found in my practice that after using FT at the end of a reprocessing session and returning to a SUDS of zero, clients are less likely to reexperience negative symptoms in between sessions as opposed to other means of closure or containment.

IN SUMMARY

There are many effective approaches that therapists can use to help clients to redefine their narratives. While the journey of trauma recovery is not a magic pill or a quick sprint through a session, there are ways of making it more tolerable and manageable for our clients. The orienting response is part of our default survival programming, but it can also be used strategically to override the impact of our past traumas. Using RDI, we can strengthen adaptive beliefs about ourselves and our ability to tolerate distress. Brainspotting, while capable of being a standalone psychotherapy in its own right, can also be a reliable means of desensitizing and resolving present stressors using focused mindfulness. And finally, the Flash Technique, though still under development, is a bilateral based intervention that rapidly provides clients with a positive outlook, granting hope toward the permanent resolution of pathogenic memories.

CHAPTER 14:

COUNTER-ATTACK: CONFRONTING OPPRESSION

The Restoration of Pride

We started the trauma history list. "Alright, are you ready to start listing out traumas?"

"I guess," the client anxiously responded. We worked hard to get to this point. He nervously laughed and slightly raised a fist, indicating that he was ready to proceed.

"OK, so we're gonna start from way back."

We listed several targets. We started with racial events from before he was born, to pre-verbal trauma that occurred while he was in the womb, to his present-day stresses. Over the course of a few sessions and using the methods listed in the previous chapter, we reprocessed events titled "Slavery in Canada" and "My Mother Did Not Want Me."

The following session, he was in tears. "David, you're not going to believe it," he said.

"What's happening?" I asked.

The client explained that after reprocessing his early preverbal traumatic memories, he no longer had a phobia of getting his partner pregnant.

"Getting your girlfriend pregnant?" I checked my notes and said, "I didn't see that phobia listed anywhere."

"That's because it wasn't!" he replied.

This was the generalization effect. He explained that by reprocessing racial trauma about the events of slavery in America, and his tumultuous birth process, he had a new lease on life. He brushed aside tears and said, "I was afraid of getting a child because I was afraid of bringing another Black child into this world."

I felt bad hearing that. It was hard to pretend not to be affected, but I shook my head and swallowed hard.

He said, "I saw all the pain that I caused my mom, and so I secretly wished never to get my girl pregnant. My girlfriend and I fought so much about this. But I couldn't bear to have another Black child cause as much pain as I caused mom."

Even if these were just events from his past that he could not necessarily put words to, the meaning he gave to them appeared to significantly impact his family and relationship.

He chuckled, leaned forward, and said, "But guess what?"

"What?" I asked.

"Just because she went through that pain, I don't have to." He straightened his back and continued, "Today, I can say I'm a proud Black man. Even if my mom had her problems, I know I can teach my kids to like themselves. Thank you for helping me to like myself again."

Trauma recovery takes courage. Under the right conditions, we can reprocess the effects of racial trauma. We all possess the innate capability of recovery. But keep in mind, our problems are not limited to the therapy session. In this chapter, we will consider suggestions for confronting oppression, inside and outside of our sessions, so we can move toward a system of change.

An Act of Resistance

In a world of White supremacy, patriarchy, homophobia, and other forms of oppression, trauma reprocessing becomes an act of resistance. Self-love becomes a form of protest. Anti-racist psychotherapy allows the person to liberate themselves from the imprisonment of adversity, social defeat, and shame. Once free from the confines of such an environment, they no longer need to accept the weight of socially constructed labels. They are always free to return, as trauma resolution does not imply a lack of free-will, but now have the choice to strive toward emancipation from mental slavery.

At the time of the opening story at the beginning of this chapter, I realized that helping a woman of any color to overcome body image issues was assisting the individual in opposing a form of gendered oppression. Talking to a gay Christian man about the sense of community he felt after coming out fights back against heterosexism and internalized homophobia. Helping my Asian clients to defend themselves against COVID-19 bullying was a way of promoting cultural pride and anti-racism. When we reprocess these traumatic memories, the changes become permanent. There is no better way to spend one's life than helping people to recognize their awesomeness.

This chapter is about specific things that all of us can do to counter the Five Faces of Oppression. The system is only set up this way because many of us are in a complicit state of homeostasis, a low-grade trance level acceptance of a status quo that does not serve anyone. If this book can help at least one person wake up and follow their calling, I will have served my purpose. Empathy is good but living with a purpose to fight for the rights of others is what will help us achieve self-determination and create a better world for all people. So here, I will invite you to commit to being on the right side of history. Let us work together and build a better future for all people.

Stored Trauma Within the White Body

DiAngelo discusses the concept of "White fragility" and what makes it so that White people have great difficulty discussing concepts such as race.[245] She explains that when discussing race, it is likely to be met with defensiveness, argument, denial, pushback, and in many cases, non-responsiveness. She explains that White people try to find ways of developing "racial stamina" to keep up with the task of embarking on the journey of managing and tolerating such socially challenging discourses. There is a push toward White people not wanting to be seen as "racist" as this would cause them to be perceived as being "bad." Hence, this "fragility" around race results in no discussion ever taking place.

Menakem suggests that the work for those who experience "white body-supremacy" is necessarily difficult, and this fragility is a part of it.[246] He outlines the contradictory myths of race that have been upheld. Black bodies are incredibly strong and dangerous; thus, they can tolerate violence to the point of destruction. This is frightening to White bodies, as White bodies are seen as vulnerable and weak. The paradox then is that these same stigmatized Black bodies are then responsible for caring for White bodies, never to disturb them, only to soothe them. He explains then that this White fragility is a trauma-driven process that is embedded deep in the nervous system. The dissociation of topics of race in our society is as deeply embedded as our dissociation from our bodies. White fragility protects against a discussion of White supremacy and hence maintains the status quo.

Menakem also explains that the journey from Europe that many White people have gone through came about due to a "flight" response. The early Europeans who traveled to the North-American continent were likely expecting a better life, as we know that generations of the medieval era, through pandemics and witch-hunting, would likely have left multigenerational trauma on large swaths of the population. It is likely that

---

[245] DiAngelo, R. (2018). *White fragility: Why it's so hard for white people to talk about racism*. Beacon Press.
[246] Menakem, R. (2017). *My Grandmother's Hands: Racialized trauma and the Pathway to Mending our Hearts and Bodies*. Central Recovery Press.

many people of European descent still have traces of the executions, lynchings, and crusades in their genetic information. There is no reason why the multigenerational transmission of trauma would not also affect the White body. But this desire to survive at all costs is maintained by the deep embedding and prioritization of Whiteness in our institutions.

Now we are confronted by the trauma of racism. Systemic racism must be reckoned with. But this must be initiated by White people because White supremacy and White fragility are two sides of the same coin.

I believe that if we are to solve the problem of racism, it begins with those who are in a position to stop it. But let us be clear, non-Black privilege exists. BIPOC who do not identify as either White or Black can still be racist toward Black people.[247] Not all White people are racist, but all non-Black people benefit from not bearing the full brunt of anti-Black racism.

We Need More Than Just Therapy

A criticism of anti-racist psychotherapy, especially the viewing of race as a socially constructed trauma or mental illness, can be likened to "psychologization."[248] Race and racial trauma must not be reduced down to solely mental illness or as another means of pathologizing the individual who suffers from White supremacy. Ndagijimana and Taffere address this, among other issues, in their groundbreaking article.[249] As progressive as we see our field, there are ways in which trauma therapists, and the various institutions which support them, contribute to neoliberalism. This deepens the wounds caused by an already oppressive system even if the desire is to make changes in the lives of our clients. The categories they discuss are the monetization of Black grief, the psychologization of poverty, and

---

[247] Badat, A. (2016). How to tackle anti-blackness as a non-black PoC. *gal-dem*. https://gal-dem.com/anti-blackness-poc-communities/
[248] DeVos, J.(2014). Psychologization. *In Encyclopedia of Critical Psychology* (pp.1547-1551). New York: Springer.
[249] Ndagijimana, J. P., & Taffere, K. (2020). Re-Envisioning Trauma Recovery: Listening and Learning From African Voices in Healing Collective Trauma. *International Journal of Human Rights Education*, 4(1), 8.

predatory inclusion, and tokenized diversity. These categories speak for themselves.

What is necessary is understanding that the problem of anti-Black racism cannot be solved by Black people alone. The problem of White supremacy cannot only be resolved by reprocessing trauma on an individual level. The sickness of a race-based society requires the work of institutions and collectives who are motivated toward transformative and absolute change. Similar to what Menakem recommends in his text[250] relating to bodywork and sustained practice, anti-racism must be seen as a mindful practice, with a willingness to confront the systems that maintain it.[251]

While there may be many methods of doing so, we will use Young's Five Faces of Oppression and provide a counterattack response. The ultimate form of defending against these forms of oppression is through complete and sustained resistance. The following are suggestions to counter the effects of a racist system in the field of psychotherapy and beyond.

Rethinking "Cultural Competence"

Cultural competence is often a phrase used in our clinical practice to express our ability to connect with others from different cultural or racial backgrounds. Its role in the therapist's pedagogy must be revisited. While useful when used in conjunction with cultural humility,[252] I mention it here for us to consider ways that its instruction and implementation can be improved.

First, it is essential for us to understand that from the outset, the term "cultural competence" is faulty. Pon criticizes this concept of cultural competence in that it appears to contribute to "new racism."[253] Rather than a

---

[250] Menakem, R. (2017). *My Grandmother's Hands: Racialized trauma and the Pathway to Mending our Hearts and Bodies*. Central Recovery Press.
[251] Kendi, I. X. (2019). *How to be an antiracist*. One World.
[252] Nickerson, M. (2017). *Cultural competence and healing culturally based trauma with EMDR therapy: Innovative strategies and protocols*. Springer Publishing Company.
[253] Pon, G. (2009). Cultural competency as new racism: An ontology of forgetting. *Journal of progressive human services, 20*(1), 59-71.

racism that is based on pseudoscientific biology, the concept invariably contributes to viewing individuals from stereotypical perspectives. This then lumps individuals into various monolithic groups, positioning them as different (and many times deficient) compared to the default of "Whiteness." Cultural competence necessitates that we "otherize" different groups without understanding the cause of their differences, whether these be socio-political occurrences, national policies, or White supremacy.

The idea of gaining competence over a client is ostentatious at best and narcissistic at worst. Pon cites Gross's article, in which the following admonition is given: aiming for "mastery of minority content may not be possible, and those who believe they have such mastery are in danger of understanding clients too soon, too superficially."[254] The therapist who focuses only on knowledge acquisition and attending as many workshops as possible on diversity is destined to preserve what Pon calls "benevolence and innocence."[255] The Western individual who is culturally competent no longer needs to engage with his or her own racist beliefs or cultural imperialistic tendencies. Where one comes from a country that has dissociated from genocide, focusing on acquired knowledge absolves one from focusing on the heart of the matter, which maintains difference. Cultural competence does not explicitly mention or challenge White supremacy as a socio-political struggle (whether internal or external to the therapist). As a concept and practice, it does not seek institutional change.

Abrams and Moio suggest that it is necessary to build upon cultural competency and cultural sensitivity training by moving toward a critical race theory perspective.[256] The authors suggest that gaining racial awareness is a process that involves "cognitive, affective, and action-oriented changes." There are no fixed skills or techniques to achieve this. However, there is a need for sustained action and continued self-reflection.

---

[254] Gross, G. D. (2000). Gatekeeping for cultural competence: Ready or not? Some post and modernist doubts. *Journal of Baccalaureate Social Work*, 5(2), 47–66.
[255] Pon, G. (2009). Cultural competency as new racism: An ontology of forgetting. *Journal of progressive human services*, 20(1), 59-71.
[256] Abrams, L. S., & Moio, J. A. (2009). Critical race theory and the cultural competence dilemma in social work education. *Journal of Social Work Education*, 45(2), 245-261.

Confronting the Five Faces of Oppression

Taking the above into account, it is now essential that we respond appropriately to the Five Faces of Oppression.

Decolonization

To defeat cultural imperialism, we must use decolonization. Sue explains that Whiteness is seen as the default within our institutions.[257] Our helping fields are no exception to this rule.[258] Decolonization is the act of realizing this and responding appropriately. Fairchild quotes Fanon[259] and explains that those who are decolonized are given the task of creating and developing a new course for humanity.[260]

In session:

Nickerson suggests that therapists are to cultivate cultural humility and to be curious when discussing race and culture.[261] Additionally, it is up to mental health professionals to be aware of the possibility of using microaggression on clients and to recognize the violent effect they can have on the recipient.

Outside of Sessions:

Therapists and other professionals have a duty and responsibility to challenge Whiteness and concepts of cultural imperialism. Knowing that this comes at a cost, it is necessary for those who seek change to organize and support like-minded individuals for the goal of community and institutional change rather than individual-level adjustments.

---

[257] Sue, D. W. (2006). The invisible whiteness of being: Whiteness, white supremacy, white privilege, and racism. In M. Constantine and D. Wing Sue (Eds.), *Addressing racism: Facilitating cultural competence in mental health and educational settings* (pp. 15–30). New Jersey: John Wiley & Sons.

[258] Pon, G. (2009). Cultural competency as new racism: An ontology of forgetting. *Journal of progressive human services, 20*(1), 59-71.

[259] Fanon, F. (1966) *The Wretched of the Earth.* New York: Grove Press

[260] Fairchild, H. H. (1994). Frantz Fanon's The Wretched of the Earth in Contemporary Perspective. *Journal of Black Studies, 25*(2), 191-199.

[261] Nickerson, M. (2017). *Cultural competence and healing culturally based trauma with EMDR therapy: Innovative strategies and protocols.* Springer Publishing Company.

Equity

To oppose exploitation, we need equity. Recognize that there is a power dynamic inherent in psychotherapy. There is one who has more power than the other. It is thus important for us to teach clients skills that encourage their independence and develop resources that counter the dependence on the therapist. As much as possible, provide a level-playing field for clients and BIPOC people alike.

In session:

Avoid gaslighting clients who tell you about difficult interactions with authority figures due to your own biases. Even if your experience with police officers differs, it is acceptable if your clients report an experience that differs from how your White-body would interact with a police-body; let us remember that Black-bodies are seen differently in our cultural context.[262] Refrain from neutralizing discussions about racism.

Outside of Sessions:

Be aware that the socio-political landscape enables the financial exploitation of Black people. Fanon often made mention that Europe was built upon (and "smothered" in) the riches of Third World countries[263]. Remember that Black people are not always paid appropriately for their services. It is not unreasonable then for White people to advocate for equity by educating and challenging donors who can make financial decisions to support Black-run community organizations.[264] Paying Black people their fair share matters.

Empowerment

To counteract powerlessness, we need empowerment. Empowerment comes from advocacy but also by boosting the lived experiences and

---

[262] Menakem, R. (2017). *My Grandmother's Hands: Racialized trauma and the Pathway to Mending our Hearts and Bodies.* Central Recovery Press.
[263] Fanon, F. (2007). *The wretched of the earth.* Grove/Atlantic, Inc.
[264] Ndagijimana, J. P., & Taffere, K. (2020). Re-Envisioning Trauma Recovery: Listening and Learning From African Voices in Healing Collective Trauma. *International Journal of Human Rights Education, 4*(1), 8.

opportunities of individuals who differ from us.

Ndagijimana and Taffere suggest that therapists consider doing more than individual counseling, as there may be a greater impact that can occur by involving the community when working with collectivist cultures.[265] Let us also value the different modes of healing of diverse communities and avoid centering on our privilege. Once in a while, offer your seat at the table to those who traditionally have power taken from them in this society.

In session:

Psychotherapy must eventually find a way of augmenting couple, family, and group therapy modalities to reduce isolation and promote community involvement. But still, in individual sessions, we can always acknowledge using the client's phraseology (when appropriate) and using their metaphoric language and imagery for resources. This can assist in cultivating a sense of pride and self-efficacy.

Outside of Sessions:

Both clients and therapists alike have a responsibility for their self-care.[266] Whether seeking psychotherapy, massage therapy, bodywork, or even some of the tools in this book, it is important for us to treat the suffering we all hold in our bodies. Managing our own internal biases reduces the chances of inadvertently disempowering our clients. And let us remember that diversity does not mean power. Raise up the voices of marginalized groups but not only as a photo-op; donating to charities is fine, but are you comfortable with donating power and influence?

Elevation

To replace marginalization, we need elevation. Elevating certain voices is an active choice. In the same way that you made an active decision to read this book, we need to improve the ability for other people

---

[265] Ndagijimana, J. P., & Taffere, K. (2020). Re-Envisioning Trauma Recovery: Listening and Learning From African Voices in Healing Collective Trauma. *International Journal of Human Rights Education, 4*(1), 8.
[266] Menakem, R. (2017). *My Grandmother's Hands: Racialized trauma and the Pathway to Mending our Hearts and Bodies.* Central Recovery Press.

of color and diverse populations to have a seat at the table. For EMDR therapy, Brainspotting, EFT, and all of the other therapeutic domains discussed in this book, there are very few (if any) trainers who are BIPOC. Despite the fact that as I explained earlier, Black people are in need of support, there is an underrepresentation of Black people in positions of influence even when it concerns our mental health.

In session:

Whatever we do not discuss will not be discussed. As a couple therapist, if the topic of sex between the partners is not brought up by the therapist, the clients will follow suit and will avoid any discussion, because that would disrupt the homeostasis of maintaining their problem. This can occur even if the client's request was initially set forward to improve romance, intimacy, or sex in the relationship—race functions in a similar way. Therapists must recognize and acknowledge racial stress; otherwise, they will inadvertently discourage clients from talking about racial trauma.[267]

Outside of Sessions:

BIPOC affinity spaces are necessary. It is necessary for us to allow for trainings where clinicians can be taught by people of color and experience a learning environment without the fear of microaggressions. Even if there are no official statistics on this, many BIPOC therapists have reported to me about both trainers and fellow participants making them uncomfortable during trainings due to culturally inappropriate or racially insensitive comments. Allowing for trainings that offer the freedom to discuss White supremacy without needing to navigate White fragility is necessary because racism affects all people's mental health. I have only been to one psychotherapy training led by a Black person, and even that person was the only BIPOC instructor in the entire world who offered trainings in that specific modality. Disappointingly, BIPOC trainers and instructors are practically nonexistent in my field. Affinity spaces are slowly becoming available, but they are not as readily promoted as some White therapists

---

[267] Ndagijimana, J. P., & Taffere, K. (2020). Re-Envisioning Trauma Recovery: Listening and Learning From African Voices in Healing Collective Trauma. *International Journal of Human Rights Education, 4*(1), 8.

have in some cases complained and attempted to discourage their operation. Institutions are completely failing us in this regard, and they must strive to do better.

Compassion

To put an end to violence, we need compassion. We must remember that when our unprocessed anger toward others is undealt with, we become the victim of it. The brain cannot easily distinguish between real and imagined stressors, and neither can the effects of cortisol on the nervous system. Increasing one's use of mindfulness is essential. Practicing generosity and gratitude is essential in a world that can be unsafe for some of us. Let us be open to knowing that we may not know it all and practice cultural humility with one another.

In session:

Let us validate the emotions that clients experience whether they face poverty or other socially engineered forms of distress. Let us avoid merely psychologizing their distress and recognize that there is a system that is unfair to those who do not fit into White male, heterosexual, able-bodied, Christian archetypes. Work on your defensiveness, learn about the necessity of anti-racism and be willing to ask hard questions and receive difficult answers.[268]

Outside of Sessions:

Understand that the fight for justice and equality will undoubtedly end up being on the right side of history. Heroes have existed in this world, heroes such as Dr. Martin Luther King Jr., Fannie Lou Hamer, Malcolm X, Fred Hampton, Huey Newton, C.T Vivian, John Lewis. Those who have attempted to obscure their messages are not the ones who will be remembered fondly in history. The lives of those who were victims of police violence have also driven us to fight for civil rights. They are ancestors who serve as heroes in a different way now. The American lives

---

[268] Ndagijimana, J. P., & Taffere, K. (2020). Re-Envisioning Trauma Recovery: Listening and Learning From African Voices in Healing Collective Trauma. *International Journal of Human Rights Education*, 4(1), 8.

of George Floyd, Breonna Taylor, Ahmaud Arbery, Tamir Rice, Michael Brown; the Canadians of different backgrounds, who may have suffered from mental health issues and lost their lives after police interventions: Ejaz Choudry, Regis Korchinski-Paquet, Sheffield Matthews; the tragic passing of Joyce Echaquan of the Atikamekw community, who died in a Quebec hospital after medical attendants mocked and insulted her on a Facebook live stream; and too many others around the world in recent years—none of these individuals have died in vain. The spirits of these individuals live on within us as one family. They grant us the courage to fight, to protect those who have been left behind, and to seek justice and change in the world. Compassion, true compassion, means taking action so that others can live without shame and suffering. Compassion means that we respond to our calling to help others to heal.

IN SUMMARY

This book ends as it started. It exists as a call to action to those who seek to improve the lives of others, to know that whether one is a therapist or not, we all have a responsibility to bring forth healing to our troubled souls who inhabit this earth. But this requires asking tough questions and seeking out tough answers. White fragility prevents discussions of White supremacy and hence maintains it. Although this book emphasizes the importance of the psychological impacts of racial trauma, our work must extend beyond the therapist's office. Anti-racism is to be enacted much like meditation is practiced—with diligence, persistence, and intention. Inside and outside of our sessions, we can commit to opposing the Five Faces of Oppression by:

- Decolonizing our vocabulary, our practice, and our actions;
- Promoting equitable practices;
- Donating power and access to others with fewer opportunities;
- Elevating the voices of those who are different from us; and
- Operating from a place of compassion.

If we all commit to one suggestion and limit the oppression of others, we can make a sustainable difference. It is not only one person's effort, but a shift in all of us, which will cause the necessary changes for tomorrow.

CHAPTER 15:

A SYSTEM OF CHANGE

Gratitude

So, congratulations. You have made it to the end of this book. I want to thank you and express my deepest gratitude that you chose to give this book a chance. I have put my heart and soul into it. It is designed to be a book that stirs the heart, stimulates the mind, and shines a beacon of light for all people who seek to seriously heal racial trauma within themselves and others.

Here is a summary of the 10 major points to remember from this book:

- Race is a social construction... and so is racial trauma.
- Anti-Black racism is a global yet common phenomenon, and, like colonization, it is an ongoing process.
- We either support racist policies or endorse anti-racist actions. Silence is complicity—meaning that neutrality does not exist.
- Racial trauma is historical, multi-generational, and reinforced in the present through media, overt violence, and covert microaggression.

- White supremacy necessitates Black suffering, and Black suffering reinforces White supremacy.
- The complex trauma of Whiteness leads White society to dissociate from their own racial trauma and avoid altering the homeostatic pattern of White supremacy/Black suffering.
- The complex trauma of Blackness stimulates White society's preoccupation with Black suffering, racial trauma, and social defeat. This maintains the homeostatic pattern of White supremacy/Black suffering.
- A family systems perspective identifies relevant actors and hierarchical structures, leading to the focus on the dynamics of interaction. This allows us to engage with forces that maintain suffering in the entire system rather than just in the "identified patient."
- Using principles of memory re-consolidation, the adaptive information processing model, and other approaches to trauma reprocessing, we can resolve deep-rooted trauma and promote healing in the nervous system.
- Our society is in the process of reconciling with race and racism. It will take time, but we must not be discouraged. We can reprocess trauma within our clients' lives, but we must start with our institutions, organizations, and ourselves first.

The importance of naming the problem is essential in couple, family, and even individual therapy. But we cannot talk about race without talking about racism. When we talk about marginalized people, we do not always discuss what keeps them marginalized. The same can be said not only for suffering but also for privilege.

Tobias and Joseph explain that when discussing White privilege on its own, there is a necessary analysis needed for White supremacy and the impact that the system has on racial minorities.[269] They explain that any discussion of Whiteness that only addresses White privilege without

---

[269] Tobias, H., & Joseph, A. (2020). Sustaining systemic racism through psychological gaslighting: Denials of racial profiling and justifications of carding by police utilizing local news media. *Race and Justice, 10(4), 424-455.*

White supremacy caters to the experience of the racial majority without addressing the experience of Black suffering. If we only talk about what one group gains, then we are avoiding (whether consciously or unconsciously) the fact that their gains are a product of what is taken from another group. It's not only that White people are gifted privilege, but that their privilege comes at the expense of the gifts taken from Black people. Hence, when we talk about anti-racism, the goal is rebalancing and restoring harmony to all members of society. This cannot be accomplished by token gestures or corporate newsletter emails plastered with #BlackLivesMatter hashtags, all while still exploiting workers. By definition, anti-racism involves the acknowledgment of an unbalanced system of operation and choosing to take deliberate and decisive action for the restoration of justice.

Strength

The goals of anti-racist psychotherapy then are to build **STRENGTH** in all people:

- Spread the use of self-care techniques and the mandate for community care.
- Teach anti-oppression as a matter of social responsibility.
- Reinforce social and economic justice for marginalized people.
- Educate the public on the effects of White supremacy on all members of our society.
- Normalize discussions of anti-Black racism as an interaction, instead of just a cause or an effect.
- Generate reliable means of self-care for those who care for others.
- Train more BIPOC and anti-racist mental health professionals, professors, and researchers.
- Highlight institutional and organizational barriers that maintain systemic racism… and be committed to change them.

This book is an attempt at clarifying the dynamic of interaction and psychological patterns that sustain racism. While my focus is on anti-Black racism, it is easy to see how other marginalized groups can also experience similar effects from oppression on a large scale. Minority stress affects all people who can be categorized as minorities. Sexuality, gender, religion, caste, Indigeneity, disability status, immigration status, socioeconomic status are all categories and labels where one can experience undue pain due to another's attribution given to them. Suffering is ordinary in our existence and I urge others who belong to these groups, to write and be inspired to write about their experience just as I have.

Courage

I believe that the founder of EMDR therapy, Francine Shapiro, might have understood this need to eliminate suffering from the world at a deep level. Unfortunately, she passed away before I could produce this manuscript; it is a sincere regret of mine that I did not meet her before she made her transition. She was a strong White woman devoted to eliminating all suffering throughout the world, regardless of race.

When I originally presented a workshop relating to the topics found in this book at the EMDR international convention, I was initially uncertain of how people would respond. I was taken aback and overwhelmed by the reception and the positive feedback received. But there was one email I received, in particular, that was special for me. It was from Dr. Steven Silver, who wrote:

It is unfortunate that Francine Shapiro died when she did. She stipulated from day one that EMDR had to be sensitive to racism and wanted to have a deliberate and active outreach to involve more [people of color] with EMDR and its development. I remember discussing this with her several times, in greatest detail in the presence of Joseph Wolpe, and we sketched out a tentative plan for doing this. Unfortunately, the attacks on EMDR, which very few of us anticipated, were so severe she had to spend much of her time and energy defending EMDR and getting it accepted - that fight isn't over but, [in my honest opinion], we can't wait for its final resolution before making EMDR inclusive. I think she would have appreciated your presentation and would have pushed to make your anti-racist orientation more of a cornerstone.

I shed a tear after reading that.

It was sad that in our pursuit of resolving the problems of trauma, mental illness, and socially induced forms of oppression that colleagues needed to fight and defend against one another. This, too, was due to maintaining power and dominance, I am sure.

But now Dr. Shapiro is an ancestor. It does not matter whether we were related or not. She is still family to me.

But that email made me reflect. Our limited time on this planet must be reserved for improving it. Colleagues, White people, Black people — none of us have time to be fighting. We need to focus on healing, if not ourselves, then the world.

Whether anyone is on the side of White supremacy or on the side of anti-racism is also of little importance when we reflect on the legacy of our lives. All labels are really responses to our negative and positive cognitions about the world around us. What's truly important is whether we can reflect on our thoughts, behaviors, and actions and honestly say we tried to make the world a little better for those who come after us. I may never be able to inspire as many as Dr. Shapiro did, but I hope that we all, as clinicians, strive to have at least half the heart that she did.

With that, I gave it my best shot. I wish to end this book by thanking you, the reader. And I thank you for keeping the conversation going. One day, we will stop the cycle of suffering and see that it was actually wisdom in the making, all along.

Blessings and Strength,

–David Archer.

INDEX

C

REFERENCES

A

Abdo, N. (2006) Sexual Violence, Patriarchy and the State: Women in Israel. *Pakistan Journal of Women's Studies*, 13 (2), 39-63.

Abrams, L. S., & Moio, J. A. (2009). Critical race theory and the cultural competence dilemma in social work education. *Journal of Social Work Education,* 45(2), 245-261.

Adam, E. K., Heissel, J. A., Zeiders, K. H., Richeson, J. A., Ross, E. C., Ehrlich, K. B., Levy, D.J., Kemeny, M., Brodish, A.B., Malanchuk, O., & Peck, S. C. (2015). Developmental histories of perceived racial discrimination and diurnal cortisol profiles in adulthood: A 20-year prospective study. *Psychoneuroendocrinology*, 62, 279-291.

Adam, E. K., Quinn, M. E., Tavernier, R., McQuillan, M. T., Dahlke, K. A., & Gilbert, K. E. (2017). Diurnal cortisol slopes and mental and physical health outcomes: A systematic review and meta-analysis. *Psychoneuroendocrinology*, 83, 25-41.

Alexander, M., Barbieri, M., & Kiang, M. (2017). Opioid deaths by race in the United States, 2000–2015. *OSF.* Retrieved December 2020 from https://osf.io/preprints/socarxiv/jm38s/download

Almeida, A. K., Macêdo, S. C. G. D. M., & Sousa, M. B. C. D. (2019). A systematic review of somatic intervention treatments in PTSD: Does Somatic Experiencing® (SE®) have the potential to be a suitable choice? *Estudos de Psicologia (Natal)*, 24(3), 237-246.

American Psychiatric Association. (2013). *Diagnostic and statistical manual of mental disorders: DSM-5.* Washington, D.C: American Psychiatric Association.

Anda, R. F., Croft, J. B., Felitti, V. J., Nordenberg, D., Giles, W. H., Williamson, D. F., & Giovino, G. A. (1999). Adverse childhood experiences and smoking during adolescence and adulthood. *Jama, 282*(17), 1652-1658.

Arcelus, J., Mitchell, A. J., Wales, J., & Nielsen, S. (2011). Mortality rates in patients with anorexia nervosa and other eating disorders: a meta-analysis of 36 studies. *Archives of general psychiatry,* 68(7), 724-731.

Archer, D. (2020). Racial Trauma, Neurons, and EMDR: The Path Towards an Anti-Racist Psychotherapy. *Go With That Magazine.*

Armstrong, M. S., & Vaughan, K. (1996). An orienting response model of eye movement desensitization. *Journal of Behavior Therapy and Experimental Psychiatry,* 27(1), 21-32.

Armstrong, N., & Vaughan, K. (1994, June). *An orienting response model for EMDR.* Paper presented at the meeting of the New South Wales Behaviour Therapy Interest Group, Sydney, Australia.

B

Badat, A. (2016). How to tackle anti-blackness as a non-black PoC. *gal-dem.* https://gal-dem.com/anti-blackness-poc-communities/

Bar-Tal, D. (1990). Causes and consequences of delegitimization: Models of conflict and ethnocentrism. *Journal of Social issues,* 46(1), 65-81

Belgrave, F. Z., & Allison, K. W. (2018). *African American psychology: From Africa to America.* Sage Publications.

Bell, D. A. (1976). Serving two masters: Integration ideals and client interests in school desegregation litigation. *The Yale Law Journal,* 85(4), 470-516.

Bell, H., Kulkarni, S., & Dalton, L. (2003). Organizational prevention of vicarious trauma. *Families in society,* 84(4), 463-470.

Berger, M., & Sarnyai, Z. (2015). "More than skin deep": stress neurobiology and mental health consequences of racial discrimination. *Stress, 18*(1), 1-10.

Bernstein, F. (2011, October 6). Derrick Bell, Law Professor and Rights Advocate, Dies at 80. *The New York Times.* https://www.nytimes.com/2011/10/06/us/derrick-bell-pioneering-harvard-law-professor-dies-at-80.html?pagewanted=all

Black (n.d.) In *Merriam-Webster's collegiate dictionary.* https://www.merriam-webster.com/dictionary/black

Bor, J., Venkataramani, A. S., Williams, D. R., & Tsai, A. C. (2018). Police killings and their spillover effects on the mental health of black Americans: a population-based, quasi-experimental study. *The Lancet, 392*(10144), 302-310.

Boyd, F. N. (1987). The Contributions of Family Therapy Models to The Treatment of Black Families. *Psychotherapy: Theory, Research, Practice, Training,* 24(3), 621-629.

Boyd, J. E., Lanius, R. A., & McKinnon, M. C. (2018). Mindfulness-based treatments for posttraumatic stress disorder: a review of the treatment literature and neurobiological evidence. *Journal of psychiatry & neuroscience: JPN, 43*(1), 7.

Bride, B. E., Robinson, M. M., Yegidis, B., & Figley, C. R. (2004). Development and validation of the secondary traumatic stress scale. *Research on social work practice, 14*(1), 27-35.

Brondolo, E., Ver Halen, N. B., Pencille, M., Beatty, D., & Contrada, R. J. (2009). Coping with racism: A selective review of the literature and a theoretical and methodological critique. *Journal of behavioral medicine, 32*(1), 64-88.

Brown, D. W., Anda, R. F., Tiemeier, H., Felitti, V. J., Edwards, V. J., Croft, J. B., & Giles, W. H. (2009). Adverse childhood experiences and the risk of premature mortality. *American journal of preventive medicine, 37*(5), 389-396.

Brown, S., & Shapiro, F. (2006). EMDR in the treatment of borderline personality disorder. *Clinical Case Studies, 5*(5), 403-420.

Brownridge, D. (2003). Male Partner Violence Against Aboriginal Women in Canada: An Empirical Analysis. *Journal of Interpersonal Violence, 18*(1), 65-83.

Brownridge, D. (2008). Understanding the Elevated Risk of Partner Violence Against Aboriginal Women: A Comparison of Two Nationally Representative Surveys of Canada. *Journal of Family Violence, 23*(5), 353-367.

Brüne, M. (2016). Borderline Personality Disorder Why 'fast and furious'? *Evolution, medicine, and public health, 2016*(1), 52-66.

Bump, P. (2020, January 8). Nearly a quarter of Americans have never experienced the U.S. in a time of peace. *The Washington Post.* https://www.washingtonpost.com/politics/2020/01/08/nearly-quarter-americans-have-never-experienced-us-time-peace/

Bunch, C. (1997). The intolerable status quo: Violence against women and girls. *The Progress of Nations, 1*, 40-49.

Burns, D. D. (1980). *Feeling good: The new mood therapy*. New York: New American Library.

C

Canetto, S. S. (2017). Suicide: Why are older men so vulnerable?. *Men and Masculinities, 20*(1), 49-70.

Capawana, M. R. (2016). Intimate attractions and sexual misconduct in the therapeutic relationship: Implications for socially just practice. *Cogent Psychology, 3*(1), 1194176.

Chapman, D. P., Whitfield, C. L., Felitti, V. J., Dube, S. R., Edwards, V. J., & Anda, R. F. (2004). Adverse childhood experiences and the risk of depressive disorders in adulthood. *Journal of affective disorders, 82*(2), 217-225.

Charpentier, A. (2017, March 19). The U.S. Has Been At War 222 Out of 239 Years. *Freakonometrics*, Hypotheses.org. https://freakonometrics.hypotheses.org/50473

Childs, E. (2004). Interracial Images: Popular Culture Depictions of Black-White Couples. *Conference Papers -- American Sociological Association*, 1-35.

Church, D., De Asis, M. A., & Brooks, A. J. (2012). Brief group intervention using Emotional Freedom Techniques for depression in college students: A randomized controlled trial. *Depression research and treatment, 2012*.

Church, D., Stern, S., Boath, E., Stewart, A., Feinstein, D., & Clond, M. (2017). Emotional freedom techniques to treat posttraumatic stress disorder in veterans: review of the evidence, survey of practitioners, and proposed clinical guidelines. *The Permanente journal, 21*.

Cieslak, R., Shoji, K., Douglas, A., Melville, E., Luszczynska, A., & Benight, C. C. (2014). A meta-analysis of the relationship between job burnout and secondary traumatic stress among workers with indirect exposure to trauma. *Psychological services, 11*(1), 75.

Comas-Diaz L., & Jacobsen F. (1993). Ethnocultural transference and counter-transference in the therapeutic dyad. *American Journal of Orthopsychiatry, 61*(3), 392-402.

Comas-Díaz, L., Hall, G. N., & Neville, H. A. (2019). Racial trauma: Theory, research, and healing: Introduction to the special issue. *American Psychologist, 74*(1), 1.

Connell, C. (2010). Multicultural Perspectives and Considerations within Structural Family Therapy: The Premises of Structure, Subsystems and Boundaries. *InSight: Rivier Academic Journal, 6*(2), 1-6.

Corrigan, F., & Grand, D. (2013). Brainspotting: Recruiting the midbrain for accessing and healing sensorimotor memories of traumatic activation. *Medical Hypotheses, 80*(6), 759-766.

D

Davis, S. D., Lebow, J. L., & Sprenkle, D. H. (2012). Common factors of change in couple therapy. *Behavior therapy, 43*(1), 36-48.

DeGruy, J. (2005). Post Traumatic Slave Syndrome. Portland: Joy De Gruy Publications Inc.

de Jongh, A., Ernst, R., Marques, L., & Hornsveld, H. (2013). The impact of eye movements and tones on disturbing memories involving PTSD and other mental disorders. *Journal of Behavior Therapy and Experimental Psychiatry, 44*(4), 477-483.

Del Giudice, M., Ellis, B. J., & Shirtcliff, E. A. (2011). The adaptive calibration model of stress responsivity. *Neuroscience & Biobehavioral Reviews, 35*(7), 1562-1592.

Delgado, R., & Stefancic, J. (2012). *Critical race theory: An introduction*. NYU Press.

Devilly, G. J., Wright, R., & Varker, T. (2009). Vicarious trauma, secondary traumatic stress or simply burnout? Effect of trauma therapy on mental health professionals. *Australian & New Zealand Journal of Psychiatry, 43*(4), 373-385.

DeVos, J.(2014). Psychologization. In *Encyclopedia of Critical Psychology* (pp.1547-1551). New York: Springer.

Di Corcia, J. A., & Tronick, E. D. (2011). Quotidian resilience: Exploring mechanisms that drive resilience from a perspective of everyday stress and coping. *Neuroscience & Biobehavioral Reviews, 35*(7), 1593-1602.

DiAngelo, R. (2018). *White fragility: Why it's so hard for white people to talk about racism*. Beacon Press.

Diaz, T. (2020, June 26). *The Skin-Lightening Industry Is Facing A Long Overdue Reckoning*. Refinery29. https://www.refinery29.com/en-ca/2020/06/9885554/skin-lightening-cream-industry-changes-companies-unilever

Dowrick, C. (2013). Depression as a culture-bound syndrome: implications for primary care. *The British Journal of General Practice, 63*(610), 229.

Dube, S. R., Anda, R. F., Felitti, V. J., Chapman, D. P., Williamson, D. F., & Giles, W. H. (2001). Childhood abuse, household dysfunction, and the risk of attempted suicide throughout the life span: findings from the Adverse Childhood Experiences Study. *Jama, 286*(24), 3089-3096.

Dudziakm M. L. (2007, May 21). New Archive: The Derrick Bell Papers. *Blogger.* https://legalhistoryblog.blogspot.com/2007/05/new-archive-derrick-bell-papers.html

Dulka, B. N., Lynch III, J. F., Latsko, M. S., Mulvany, J. L., & Jasnow, A. M. (2015). Phenotypic responses to social defeat are associated with differences in cued and contextual fear discrimination. *Behavioural processes, 118*, 115-122.

Dutt, T. (2020, September 17). Feeling Like an Outcast. *Foreign Policy.* https://foreignpolicy.com/2020/09/17/caste-book-india-dalit-outcast-wilkerson-review/

E

Ecker, B., Ticic, R., & Hulley, L. (2012). *Unlocking the emotional brain: Eliminating symptoms at their roots using memory reconsolidation.* Routledge.

EMDRIA. (n.d.) *Experiencing EMDR Therapy.* https://www.emdria.org/about-emdr-therapy/experiencing-emdr-therapy/

Encyclopaedia Britannica. (n.d.). Critical race theory: Additional Information. In *Encyclopaedia Britannica.com. Retrieved December 14, 2020* from https://www.britannica.com/topic/critical-race-theory

Eom, Y. H., Aragón, P., Laniado, D., Kaltenbrunner, A., Vigna, S., & Shepelyansky, D. L. (2015). Interactions of cultures and top people of Wikipedia from ranking of 24 language editions. *PloS one, 10*(3), e0114825.

Epstein, M. (1995). *Thoughts without a thinker*. New York: Basic Books.

Espinoza, R. K., & Ek, B. J. (2011). An Examination of Juveniles Being Tried As Adults: Influences of Ethnicity, Socioeconomic Status and Age of Defendant. *National Social Science Journal, 37*(1), 30-37.

F

Fairchild, H. H. (1994). Frantz Fanon's The Wretched of the Earth in Contemporary Perspective. *Journal of Black Studies*, 25(2), 191-199.

Fanon, F. (1970). *Black skin, white masks* (pp. 13-30). London: Paladin.

Fanon, F. (2007). *The wretched of the earth*. Grove/Atlantic, Inc.

Feinstein, D. (1990). Transference and countertransference in the here-and-now therapies. *Hakomi Forum*, 1(8), 7-13.

Felitti, V. J. (2009). Adverse childhood experiences and adult health. *Academic Pediatrics, 9*(3), 131-132.

Felitti, V. J., Anda, R. F., Nordenberg, D., Williamson, D. F., Spitz, A. M., Edwards, V., & Marks, J. S. (1998). Relationship of childhood abuse and household dysfunction to many of the leading causes of death in adults: The Adverse Childhood Experiences (ACE) Study. *American journal of preventive medicine, 14*(4), 245-258.

Ford, J. D., Stockton, P., Kaltman, S., & Green, B. L. (2006). Disorders of extreme stress (DESNOS) symptoms are associated with type and severity of interpersonal trauma exposure in a sample of healthy young women. *Journal of Interpersonal Violence, 21*(11), 1399-1416.

Freeman, H. (1991). Race, poverty, and cancer. *Journal of the National Cancer Institute, 83*, 526-527.

Fuzikawa, C. (2015). Brainspotting: uma nova abordagem psicoterápica para o tratamento do trauma. *Revista Debates em Psiquiatria, 3*, 26-30. Retrieved from http://abpbrasil.websiteseguro.com/portal/wp-content/upload/rdp_15/03/RDP_3_2015_geral1.pdf

G

Gilbert, J. (2006). Cultural imperialism revisited: Counselling and globalisation. *International Journal of Critical Psychology, 17*, 10-28.

Gordon, K. H., Castro, Y., Sitnikov, L., & Holm-Denoma, J. M. (2010). Cultural body shape ideals and eating disorder symptoms among White, Latina, and Black college women. *Cultural Diversity and Ethnic Minority Psychology, 16*(2), 135.

Grand, D. (2013). *Brainspotting: The revolutionary new therapy for rapid and effective change.* Sounds True.

Gregory, R. J., Schwer Canning, S., Lee, T. W., & Wise, J. C. (2004). Cognitive Bibliotherapy for Depression: A Meta-Analysis. *Professional Psychology: Research and Practice, 35*(3), 275.

Grencavage, L. M., & Norcross, J. C. (1990). Where are the commonalities among the therapeutic common factors?. Professional psychology: *Research and practice, 21*(5), 372.

Grier, W. H., & Cobbs, P. M. (2000). *Black rage.* Wipf and Stock Publishers.

Grills, C. T. (2004). African psychology. In R. L. Jones (Ed.), *Black psychology* (4th ed.). Hampton, VA: Cobb & Henry.

Gross, G. D. (2000). Gatekeeping for cultural competence: Ready or not? Some post and modernist doubts. *Journal of Baccalaureate Social Work, 5*(2), 47–66.

Gurda, K. (2015). Emerging trauma therapies: Critical analysis and discussion of three novel approaches. *Journal of Aggression, Maltreatment & Trauma, 24*(7), 773-793.

H

Hall, G. (2012, March 8). Derrick A. Bell: Who's Afraid of Critical Race Theory? *Blogger.* https://lawdawghall.blogspot.com/2012/03/derrick-bell-whos-afraid-of-critical.html

Hart, W. (2011). *The art of living: Vipassana meditation as taught by SN Goenka.* Pariyatti.

Hauptman, L. M. (2008). *Seven generations of Iroquois leadership: The six nations since 1800.* Syracuse University Press.

Herbenick, D., van Anders, S. M., Brotto, L. A., Chivers, M. L., Jawed-Wessel, S., & Galarza, J. (2019). Sexual harassment in the field of sexuality research. *Archives of sexual behavior, 48*(4), 997-1006.

Herman, J. (1992). *Trauma and Recovery.* New York: Basic Books.

Hildebrand A., Grand, D., Stemmler, M., (n.d.) A preliminary study of the efficacy of Brainspotting –a new therapy for the treatment of Posttraumatic Stress Disorder. *Journal for Psychotraumatology, Psychotherapy Science and Psychological Medicin.* Retrieved from: https://brainspotting.com/wp-content/uploads/2018/02/Hildebrand-Grand-and-Stemmler-2014-Jrnl-Psyctrau-PsyctherSci-Pysclgcl-Med20.pdf

Hildebrand, A., Grand, D., & Stemmler, M. (2017). Brainspotting–the efficacy of a new therapy approach for the treatment of Posttraumatic Stress Disorder in comparison to Eye Movement Desensitization and Reprocessing. *Mediterranean Journal of Clinical Psychology, 5*(1).

Hinton, D. E., & Simon, N. (2015). Toward a Cultural Neuroscience of Anxiety Disorders: The Multiplex Model. In L. Kirmayer, R. Lemelson, & C. Cummings (Eds.), *Re-Visioning Psychiatry: Cultural Phenomenology, Critical Neuroscience, and Global Mental Health* (pp. 343-374). Cambridge: Cambridge University Press. doi:10.1017/CBO9781139424745.017

Hogan, L. (2016, November 7). Two years of the 'Irish slaves' myth: racism, reductionism and the tradition of diminishing the transatlantic slave trade. *openDemocracy*. https://www.opendemocracy.net/en/beyond-trafficking-and-slavery/two-years-of-irish-slaves-myth-racism-reductionism-and-tradition-of-diminis/

Hutson, J. A., Taft, J. G., Barocas, S., & Levy, K. (2018). Debiasing desire: Addressing bias & discrimination on intimate platforms. *Proceedings of the ACM on Human-Computer Interaction, 2*(CSCW), 1-18.

I

Isobel, S., & Angus-Leppan, G. (2018). Neuro-reciprocity and vicarious trauma in psychiatrists. *Australasian Psychiatry, 26*(4), 388-390.

Ivey-Stephenson, A. Z., Crosby, A. E., Jack, S. P., Haileyesus, T., & Kresnow-Sedacca, M. J. (2017). Suicide trends among and within urbanization levels by sex, race/ethnicity, age group, and mechanism of death—United States, 2001–2015. *MMWR Surveillance Summaries, 66*(18), 1.

J

James, G. G. (2013). Stolen legacy. Simon and Schuster

Jeffries, F. W., & Davis, P. (2013). What is the role of eye movements in eye movement desensitization and reprocessing (EMDR) for post-traumatic stress disorder (PTSD)? A review. *Behavioural and cognitive psychotherapy, 41*(3), 290.

Johansson, P. M., & Punzi, E. (2019). Jewishness and psychoanalysis-the relationship to identity, trauma and exile. An interview study. *Jewish Culture and History, 20*(2), 140-152.

Johnson, P. (2003, October 12). The oldest form of racism. *The Telegraph.* https://www.telegraph.co.uk/culture/books/3604398/The-oldest-form-of-racism.html

Johnson, M. P. & Ferraro, K. J. (2000), Research on Domestic Violence in the 1990s: Making Distinctions. *Journal of Marriage and Family, 62*, 948–963.

Jones, E. E. (2018, July 8). Why are memes of black people reacting so popular online?. *The Guardian.* https://www.theguardian.com/culture/2018/jul/08/why-are-memes-of-black-people-reacting-so-popular-online

Juster, R. P., McEwen, B. S., & Lupien, S. J. (2010). Allostatic load biomarkers of chronic stress and impact on health and cognition. *Neuroscience & Biobehavioral Reviews, 35*(1), 2-16.

K

Kabat-Zinn, J. (2003), Mindfulness-Based Interventions in Context: Past, Present, and Future. *Clinical Psychology: Science and Practice, 10*, 144–156.

Kao, G. (2000). Group Images and Possible Selves Among Adolescents: Linking Stereotypes to Expectations by Race and Ethnicity. *Sociological Forum, 15*(3), 407-730.

Kate, M. A., Jamieson, G., Dorahy, M. J., & Middleton, W. (2020). Measuring Dissociative Symptoms and Experiences in an Australian College Sample Using a Short Version of the Multidimensional Inventory of Dissociation. *J Trauma Dissociation*, 1-23.

Kelly, S., Maynigo, P., Wesley, K., & Durham, J. (2013). African American communities and family systems: Relevance and challenges. Couple and Family Psychology: *Research and Practice, 2*(4), 264.

Kemeny, M., Brodish, A.B., Malanchuk, O. and Peck, S.C., (2015). Developmental histories of perceived racial discrimination and diurnal cortisol profiles in adulthood: A 20-year prospective study. *Psychoneuroendocrinology, 62, 279-291.*

Kendi, I. X. (2019). *How to be an antiracist.* One World.

King, T. (2017). *The inconvenient Indian illustrated: A curious account of native people in North America.* Doubleday Canada.

Knefel, M., Lueger-Schuster, B., Karatzias, T., Shevlin, M., & Hyland, P. (2019). From child maltreatment to ICD-11 complex post-traumatic stress symptoms: The role of emotion regulation and re-victimisation. *Journal of clinical psychology, 75*(3), 392-393.

Kucsera, J.V. (2009). *Racial Mindfulness : Exploring the Influence of Mindfulness on Racial Biases* (Doctoral dissertation). Retrieved from UT Electronic Theses and Dissertations.

L

Lavergne, C., Dufour, S., Trocmé, N. & Larrivée, M.-C. (2008). Visible Minority, Aboriginal and Caucasians Children investigated by Canadian Child protective services. *Child Welfare, 87*(2), 59-76.

Le, T. N., & Stockdale, G. (2008). Acculturative Dissonance, Ethnic Identity, and Youth Violence. Cultural Diversity & Ethnic Minority Psychology, 14(1), 1-9.

Leeds, A. M. (2016). *A guide to the standard EMDR therapy protocols for clinicians, supervisors, and consultants. Springer Publishing Company.* 2nd edition. New York: Springer Publishing Company

Lester, P. (2012, August 30). Stevie Wonder: 'I never thought of being blind and black as a disadvantage'. *The Guardian.* https://www.theguardian.com/music/2012/aug/30/stevie-wonder-blind-black-disadvantage

Levine, P. A. (2015). *Trauma and memory: Brain and body in a search for the living past: A practical guide for understanding and working with traumatic memory.* North Atlantic Books.

Light, A., & Strayer, W. (2002). From Bakke To Hopwood: Does Race Affect College Attendance and Completion? *Review of Economics & Statistics, 84*(1), 34-45.

Lillis J., Hayes S.C. (2007). Applying acceptance, mindfulness, and values to the reduction of prejudice: a pilot study. *Behavior modification, 31*(4) , pp. 389-411.

Lipke, H. (1992). *Manual for the teaching of Shapiro's EMDR in the treatment of combat related PTSD.* Pacific Grove, CA: EMDR Institute.

Lipke, H. (1999). *EMDR and psychotherapy integration: Theoretical and clinical suggestions with focus on traumatic stress.* Boca Raton, FL: CRC Press.

Lock, J. & Le Grange, D. (2015). *Treatment manual for anorexia nervosa: A family-based approach.* Guilford Publications.

Lock, J., & Le Grange, D. (2015a). *Help your teenager beat an eating disorder.* Guilford Publications.

Lock, J., & Le Grange, D. (2015b). *Treatment manual for anorexia nervosa: A family-based approach.* Guilford Publications.

Luber, M., & Shapiro, F. (2009). Interview with Francine Shapiro: Historical overview, present issues, and future directions of EMDR. *Journal of EMDR Practice and Research, 3*(4), 217-231.

Luk, V. (2020, May 31). *How Filipino-Canadian care aides are disproportionately affected by the COVID-19 pandemic.* CBC. https://www.cbc.ca/news/canada/british-columbia/covid-19-filipino-care-aides-affected-1.5589603

M

MacCulloch, M. J., & Feldman, P. (1996). Eye movement desensitisation treatment utilises the positive visceral element of the investigatory reflex to inhibit the memories of post-traumatic stress disorder: a theoretical analysis. *The British Journal of Psychiatry, 169*(5), 571-579.

Malcolm, X. (2015). *The Autobiography of Malcolm X.* Ballantine Books.

Manfield, P., Lovett, J., Engel, L., & Manfield, D. (2017). Use of the flash technique in EMDR therapy: Four case examples. *Journal of EMDR Practice and Research, 11*(4), 195-205.

Masson, J., Bernoussi, A., & Moukouta, C. S. (2017). Brainspotting Therapy: About a Bataclan Victim. *Global Journal of Health Science, 9*(7).

Maté, G. (2008). *In the realm of hungry ghosts: Close encounters with addiction.* Random House Digital, Inc.

Matthijssen, S. J., van Schie, K., & van den Hout, M. A. (2018). The Effect of modality specific interference on working memory in recalling aversive auditory and visual memories. *Cognition and Emotion.*

Mays, V. M., Cochran, S. D., & Barnes, N. W. (2007). Race, race-based discrimination, and health outcomes among African Americans. *Annu. Rev. Psychol., 58*, 201-225.

McEwen, B. S. (1998). Stress, adaptation, and disease: Allostasis and allostatic load. *Annals of the New York academy of sciences, 840*(1), 33-44.

McEwen, B. S. (2006). Protective and damaging effects of stress mediators: central role of the brain. *Dialogues in clinical neuroscience, 8*(4), 367.

McGoldrick, M., Gerson, R., & Petry, S. S. (2008). *Genograms: Assessment and intervention.* WW Norton & Company.

McHugh, P. P. (2017). The impact of compensation, supervision and work design on internship efficacy: implications for educators, employers and prospective interns. *Journal of Education and Work, 30*(4), 367-382.

Menakem, R. (2017). *My Grandmother's Hands: Racialized trauma and the Pathway to Mending our Hearts and Bodies.* Central Recovery Press.

Miller W. R., Rollnick, S. (2002). *Motivational Interviewing: Preparing People for Change.* New York: Guilford Press, p.39.

Miller, W. R., & Rollnick, S. (2009). Ten things that motivational interviewing is not. *Behavioural and cognitive psychotherapy, 37*(2), 129-140.

Miller, W. R., & Rollnick, S. (2012). *Motivational interviewing: Helping people change.* Guilford Press.

Mohamed, C. & Smith, R. (1999). Race in the therapy relationship. In M. Lawrence, M. Maguire & J. Campling (Eds.), *Psychotherapy with women: feminist perspectives* (pp. 134-159). New York: Routledge.

Mosquera, D., Leeds, A. M., & Gonzalez, A. (2014). Application of EMDR therapy for borderline personality disorder. *Journal of EMDR Practice and Research, 8*(2), 74-89.

Mullaly, B. (2010a). *Internalized Oppression and Domination. Challenging Oppression and Confronting Privilege* (160-187). Don Mills, ON: Oxford University Press.

Mullaly, B. (2010b). *Oppression at the Cultural Level. Challenging Oppression and Confronting Privilege* (93-125). Don Mills, ON: Oxford University Press.

Müller-Wille, S. (2014). Linnaeus and the Four Corners of the World. In *The Cultural Politics of Blood, 1500–1900* (pp. 191-209). Palgrave Macmillan, London.

N

National Archives of Canada, Record Group 10, vol. 6810, file 470-2-3, vol. 7, 55 (L-3) and 63 (N-3).

Ndagijimana, J. P., & Taffere, K. (2020). Re-Envisioning Trauma Recovery: Listening and Learning From African Voices in Healing Collective Trauma. *International Journal of Human Rights Education, 4*(1), 8.

Nickerson, M. (2017). *Cultural competence and healing culturally based trauma with EMDR therapy: Innovative strategies and protocols.* Springer Publishing Company

Nosek, B. A., Greenwald, A. G., & Banaji, M. R. (2005). Understanding and using the Implicit Association Test II: Method variables and construct validity. *Personality and Social Psychology Bulletin, 31*,166–180.

O

O'Brien, K. J. (2007) *The Uncounted Casualties of War: Epigenetics and the Intergenerational Transference of PTSD Symptoms among Children and Grandchildren of Vietnam Veterans in Australia.* https://eprints.qut.edu.au/13794/1/13794.pdf, accessed November 11, 2020.

OER Services. (n.d.) *The Caste System.*
https://courses.lumenlearning.com/suny-hccc-worldcivilization/chapter/the-caste-system/

P

Patrícia F.M., José F.P., de F and Marcelo M (2015) Persistent Genital Arousal Disorder as a Dissociative Trauma Related Condition Treated with Brainspotting – A Successful Case Report *Int J Sch Cog Psychol S1*: 002 Retrieved December 15, 2020 from https://brainspotting.com/wp-content/uploads/2018/02/Ferreira-Mattos-et-al-2015-IntlJrnlofSchandCogPsych-CaseRpt-S1.pdf

Pearce, J., Rafiq, S., Simpson, J., & Varese, F. (2019). Perceived discrimination and psychosis: a systematic review of the literature. *Social Psychiatry and Psychiatric Epidemiology*, 1-22.

Perroud, N., Rutembesa, E., Paoloni-Giacobino, A., Mutabaruka, J., Mutesa, L., Stenz, L., & Karege, F. (2014). The Tutsi genocide and transgenerational transmission of maternal stress: epigenetics and biology of the HPA axis. *The World Journal of Biological Psychiatry, 15*(4), 334-345.

Pon, G. (2009). Cultural competency as new racism: An ontology of forgetting. *Journal of progressive human services, 20*(1), 59-71

R

Ray W. (2018) The Palo Alto Group. In: Lebow J., Chambers A., Breunlin D. (eds) *Encyclopedia of Couple and Family Therapy.* Springer, Cham. https://doi.org/10.1007/978-3-319-15877-8_596-1

Repetti, R. L., Taylor, S. E., & Seeman, T. E. (2002). Risky families: Family social environments and the mental and physical health of offspring. *Psychological Bulletin, 128*, 330-366.

Roberts, T., & Andrews, D. C. (2013). *A critical race analysis of the gaslighting against African American teachers considerations for recruitment and retention.* In D. C. Andrews (Ed.), Contesting the myth of a "post racial" era: The continued significance of race in U.S. Education (Black Studies and Critical Thinking) (1st ed., pp. 69–94). New York, NY: Peter Lang.

Rockinson-Szapkiw, A. J., Payne, L. Z., & West, L. C. (2011). Leadership lessons from Salvador Minuchin. *The Family Journal,* 19(2), 191-197.

Rutherford, A. (2020). *How to Argue with a Racist: History, Science, Race and Reality.* Hachette UK.

S

Salter, M., & Hall, H. (2020). Reducing shame, promoting dignity: a model for the primary prevention of complex post-traumatic stress disorder. *Trauma, Violence, & Abuse,* 1524838020979667.

Satir, V. (1988). *The New Peoplemaking.* New York. Science and Behavior Books, Inc.

Schwartz, H. L. (2013). *The alchemy of wolves and sheep: A relational approach to internalized perpetration in complex trauma survivors.* Routledge.

Sebastian, B., & Nelms, J. (2017). The effectiveness of Emotional Freedom Techniques in the treatment of posttraumatic stress disorder: A meta-analysis. *Explore, 13*(1), 16-25.

Seliga, M. (2009). Empirically supported treatment interventions for clients with posttraumatic stress disorder and comorbid borderline personality disorder: A critical review. *Where Reflection & Practice Meet The Changing Nature of Social Work: Towards Global Practice.*

Selten, J. P., van der Ven, E., Rutten, B. P., & Cantor-Graae, E. (2013). The social defeat hypothesis of schizophrenia: an update. *Schizophrenia bulletin, 39*(6), 1180-1186.

Shade, L. R., & Jacobson, J. (2015). Hungry for the job: gender, unpaid internships, and the creative industries. *The Sociological Review, 63*(S1), 188-205.

Shah, S. (2020). The US Has Been at war 225 out of 243 years since 1776. *The News International.* https://www.thenews.com.pk/print/595752-the-us-has-been-at-war-225-out-of-243-years-since-1776

Shapiro, F. (2017). *Eye movement desensitization and reprocessing (EMDR) therapy: Basic principles, protocols, and procedures.* Guilford Publications.

Shengold, L. (1991). *Soul murder: The effects of childhood abuse and deprivation.* BoD–Books on Demand.

Shepherd, R. (2019). The Relationship Between the Repeated Social Defeat Stress Experimental Model, Delegitimization, and Neuroresilience in Experiences of Young African-American Males. *Journal of Underrepresented & Minority Progress, 3*(2), 99-108.

Siegel, D. J. (2012). *The developing mind: How relationships and the brain interact to shape who we are (2nd ed.).* New York, NY: Guilford Press.

Smith, A. (2012). Indigeneity, settler colonialism, white supremacy. *Racial formation in the twenty-first century*, 66.

Solomon, R. M., & Shapiro, F. (2008). EMDR and the adaptive information processing model potential mechanisms of change. Journal of EMDR practice and Research, 2(4), 315-325.

Sprenkle, D. H., & Blow, A. J. (2004). Common factors and our sacred models. *Journal of marital and family therapy, 30*(2), 113-129.

Steinmetz, K. (2020). She Coined the Term 'Intersectionality' Over 30 Years Ago. Here's What It Means to Her Today. *Time.* https://time.com/5786710/kimberle-crenshaw-intersectionality/

Stroud, L. R., Salovey, P., & Epel, E. S. (2002). Sex differences in stress responses: social rejection versus achievement stress. *Biological psychiatry, 52*(4), 318-327.

Sue, D. W. (2006). The invisible whiteness of being. Whiteness, white supremacy, white privilege, and racism. In M. Constantine and D. Wing Sue (Eds.), *Addressing racism: Facilitating cultural competence in mental health and educational settings* (pp. 15–30). New Jersey: John Wiley & Sons.

Sue, D. W., Capodilupo, C. M., Torino, G. C., Bucceri, J. M., Holder, A., Nadal, K. L., & Esquilin, M. (2007). Racial microaggressions in everyday life: implications for clinical practice. *American psychologist, 62*(4), 271

T

Tamblyn, T. (2014, June 12). Wikipedia Reveals Most Influential Person In History, No It's Not Jesus. *The Huffington Post.* https://www.huffingtonpost.co.uk/2014/06/12/wikipedia-most-influential-person-jesus_n_5487516.html

Taylor, S. E., & Stanton, A. L. (2007). Coping resources, coping processes, and mental health. *Annu. Rev. Clin. Psychol., 3*, 377-401.

The Washington Post. (2020) *Fatal Force [Database that records police shootings in the United States].* Retrieved December 14, 2020 from https://www.washingtonpost.com/graphics/investigations/police-shootings-database/

Titelman, P. (Ed.). (2014). *Differentiation of self: Bowen family systems theory perspectives.* Routledge.

Tobias, H., & Joseph, A. (2020). Sustaining systemic racism through psychological gaslighting: Denials of racial profiling and justifications of carding by police utilizing local news media. *Race and Justice, 10*(4), 424-455.

Todd, N. R., & Abrams, E. M. (2011). White dialectics: A new framework for theory, research, and practice with White students. *The Counseling Psychologist, 39*, 353-395.

Trippany, R. L., Kress, V. E. W., & Wilcoxon, S. A. (2004). Preventing vicarious trauma: What counselors should know when working with trauma survivors. *Journal of Counseling & Development, 82*(1), 31-37.

Tummala-Narra, P. (2007). Skin color and the therapeutic relationship. *Psychoanalytic Psychology, 24*(2), 255-270.

U

United States Census Bureau. (2018, September 6). *Older People Projected to Outnumber Children for First Time in U.S. History.* Retrieved December 14, 2020 from https://www.census.gov/newsroom/press-releases/2018/cb18-41-population-projections.html

V

van der Kolk, B. A. (1996). The body keeps score: Approaches to the psychobiology of posttraumatic stress disorder. In B. A. van der Kolk, A. C. McFarlane, & L. Weisaeth (Eds.), *Traumatic stress: The effects of overwhelming experience on mind, body, and society* (pp. 214–241). The Guilford Press.

van der Kolk, B. A. (2015). *The body keeps the score: Brain, mind, and body in the healing of trauma.* Penguin Books.

W

Wampold, B. E. (2015). How important are the common factors in psychotherapy? An update. *World Psychiatry, 14*(3), 270-277.

Warren, B. L., Vialou, V. F., Iñiguez, S. D., Alcantara, L. F., Wright, K. N., Feng, J., Kennedy, P.J., LaPlant, Q., Shen, L., Nestler, E.J., & Bolaños-Guzmán, C. A. (2013). Neurobiological sequelae of witnessing stressful events in adult mice. *Biological psychiatry*, *73*(1), 7-14.

Welsing, F. C. (1991). *The Isis (Yssis) papers*. Chicago, IL: Third World Press.

White (n.d.) In *Merriam-Webster's collegiate dictionary*. https://www.merriam-webster.com/dictionary/black

Williams, A., Oliver, C., Aumer, K., & Meyers, C. (2016). Racial microaggressions and perceptions of Internet memes. *Computers in Human Behavior, 63*, 424-432.

Williams, D. R. (1999), Race, Socioeconomic Status, and Health: The Added Effects of Racism and Discrimination. Annals of the New York Academy of Sciences, 896, 173–188.

Williams, M. T. (2019). Adverse racial climates in academia: Conceptualization, interventions, and call to action. *New ideas in Psychology, 55*, 58-67.

Williams, M. T. (2019, February 13). Uncovering the Trauma of Racism. *American Psychological Association*. https://www.apa.org/pubs/highlights/spotlight/issue-128

Wolff, R., & Barsamian, D. (2012). *Occupy the economy: Challenging capitalism*. City Lights Books.

World Health Organization. (2013, August 6). *WHO releases guidance on mental health care after trauma*. Retrieved December 20, 2020 from: https://www.who.int/mediacentre/news/releases/2013/trauma_menta l_health_20130806/en/

Wright, B. R. E., & Younts, C. W. (2009). Reconsidering the relationship between race and crime: Positive and negative predictors of crime among African American youth. *Journal of Research in Crime and Delinquency, 46*(3), 327-352.

Y

Yehuda, R., Daskalakis, N. P., Bierer, L. M., Bader, H. N., Klengel, T., Holsboer, F., & Binder, E. B. (2016). Holocaust exposure induced intergenerational effects on FKBP5 methylation. *Biological psychiatry, 80*(5), 372-380.

Yehuda, R., Engel, S. M., Brand, S. R., Seckl, J., Marcus, S. M., & Berkowitz, G. S. (2005). Transgenerational effects of posttraumatic stress disorder in babies of mothers exposed to the World Trade Center attacks during pregnancy. *The Journal of Clinical Endocrinology & Metabolism, 90*(7), 4115-4118.

Young, I. M. (2000). Five faces of oppression. In M. Adams, W. J. Blumenfeld, R.Castaneda, H. W. Hackman, M. L. Peters, & X. Zuniga (Eds.), *Readings for diversity and social justice: An anthology on racism, antisemitism, sexism, heterosexism, ableism and classism* (pp. 35-49). New York: Routledge.

Yuan, S., Zhou, X., Zhang, Y., Zhang, H., Pu, J., Yang, L., Liu L., Jiang, X., & Xie, P. (2018). Comparative efficacy and acceptability of bibliotherapy for depression and anxiety disorders in children and adolescents: a meta-analysis of randomized clinical trials. *Neuropsychiatric disease and treatment, 14*, 353.

LET'S WORK TOGETHER

David Archer is available for podcasts, presentations, and trainings.

**Let's deliver the message of Anti-Racist Psychotherapy
to those who need it.**

Email me at david@archertherapy.com for more information.

In closing, free resources and videos are available on my website
www.antiracistpsychotherapy.com.

You are invited to view and download these free resources.
Be well, stay healthy, and take care.

CPSIA information can be obtained
at www.ICGtesting.com
Printed in the USA
LVHW102149151222
735339LV00026B/786